MW01487951

Carry On Like You Live

Copyright © 2018 John Adams
All Rights Reserved.
ISBN-13: 978-1725971578
ISBN-10: 1725971577
CreateSpace Independent Publishing Platform
North Charleston, SC
All rights reserved. Manufactured in the United States of America.
First printing, 2018
Cover design and illustration: Daniel Proctor
Book design and layout: Mary Ann Venable

Table of Contents

Acknowledgements

I started writing for publication when I was only 15 years old. And not until last January did I even consider writing a book.

When you have written five sports columns a week for decades, you aren't looking to spend more time at a computer keyboard.

That changed in January. The death of my good friend, Randy Peay, a month earlier was the catalyst.

I was so saddened by his loss that I wrote a column about him for my newspaper and web site. That took me back to a different time – a better time, perhaps. It also took me back to my hometown.

People like Randy are what made Clinton so endearing to me. And writing about him put me back in Clinton.

It also made me realize that I missed more than Randy.

My wife, Melinda, had encouraged me to write a book about Clinton after she first visited my hometown and immediately became so enthralled with it.

This book was a collaborative effort. And the first collaborators were Melinda and my friend and former neighbor, Catherine Landry, who repeatedly told me I should consider writing a book on Clinton.

But even as I took the first steps toward writing the book, I wasn't sure they would lead to a completed manuscript.

That's where so many other collaborators came in. Each interview gave me more than anecdotes. It gave me additional incentive.

In fact, the interviewees seemingly wanted the book as much as I did. After all, it was their hometown, too. One interview led to another until I realized a project that seemed so uncertain when it began was quite doable.

But it wasn't just my project. It was our project.

And the best part of it was renewing acquaintances with so many people from my past. Reconnecting with childhood friends and acquaintances wasn't awkward at all. Our shared memories and experiences made it easy. Wonderfully so.

I wrote about many of those people. I can't thank them enough for giving so much of their time, often through long telephone interviews.

I talked to my lifelong friend, Mike Felps, as much as anyone about this book. I wasn't halfway through when he died in March. His loss, coupled with Randy's a few months earlier, sometimes left me writing through tears. But then, I would catch myself and imagine Mike and Randy reading these stories and adding to them with stories of their own. I would remember how much they made me laugh, and write on.

I wasn't as close to former classmates Odie Gonsoulin and Billy Perkins, who are the subjects of one chapter. But I could empathize with them.

All three of us were in the Army during the Vietnam War. By the luck of the draw, I edited the post paper in Fort Riley, Kan.; they heroically fought their way through an almost impossible situation and paid a terrible price for it. I was so sorry for what they went through but so proud of what they did.

I mentioned Roland and Malva Huson, co-owners of The Watchman, in a couple of chapters. They gave me my first newspaper job, for which I'm ever grateful.

Most of all, I want to thank my mother, Marie Adams, who raised me as a single parent at the same time she was caring for her elderly mother. She was a blessing to have as a mother and a joy to be around.

And she loved Clinton as much as I do.

Foreword

John Dean was always late for school. I remember him racing across his front lawn, books tucked at his side, as I watched from across the street.

He was on his way to Clinton High School where not only was he furthering his education, but forming lifelong friendships and - unbeknownst to him - gathering material for this long awaited book.

His wife, Melinda, and I have told him for years that he should write a book about Clinton. Finally, the timing was right, and the wealth of information he gathered has been worth the wait. John Dean has interviewed over 100 people, whose stories have made this book so compelling.

As I read about the goings on of Clinton, I thought anyone who grew up in a small town could identify with the people he has written about. They watched out for you and taught lessons that carried you through life's challenges.

A great football player couldn't reach his potential because of injuries but later became a success in business. Another great football player overcame a lack of size to surpass his potential. A bright, sweet girl with a menacing vision condition would go on to raise four children and inspire people in her unwavering faith. A young World War II bride would have the courage and commitment to move far from home and build a new life comprised of family and business.

John Dean brings us down Main Street where there once were thriving businesses and the never-ending bustle around the Courthouse Square. He takes us down side streets, too - through his neighborhood and beyond.

You can imagine yourself sitting in the bleachers on a cool fall night watching a Clinton High football game. John Dean doesn't just tell you about the coaches and players. He reminds you how big a high school football game could be in a small town. An award-winning sportswriter who has covered the biggest sporting events in the world, he hasn't forgotten where it all starts.

He's not writing so much about a place, as he is the people who made the place so special.

Even Hollywood recognized the beauty of Clinton. It brought Paul Newman and Joanne Woodward together for "The Long Hot Summer." After they burst on to the Clinton scene in 1957, other stars and movies followed.

Our beautiful architecture and scenic rolling hills have been in movies and on TV for over fifty years. Our movie legacy is strong and enduring. But the real Clinton - the one of our childhood - was even stronger.

Communities change. People move in and out.

But in our mind's eye, our hometown hasn't changed at all. It remains a special place.

This book reminds us just how special.

Catherine L. Landry
Clinton, Louisiana

The Traveling Gene

Sunday trips in the fall have been difficult throughout my sports writing career. But when I left Knoxville, Tenn., on a Sunday in 1994, I had no inkling that the trip to Atlanta would end up being the most difficult of all.

For much of my career as a sports columnist, a typical weekend had consisted of a college game on Saturday and an NFL game on Sunday. When I was at the Clarion Ledger in Jackson, Miss., in the late 1970s, I would cover an Ole Miss or Mississippi State game on Saturday, then drive three hours to New Orleans the following morning for a Saints game.

In Jacksonville, Fla., I might have covered a Florida, Florida State or Georgia game on Saturday and a Falcons or Tampa Bay Bucs game on Sunday. In Knoxville, after covering a Tennessee game, I might have driven to Cincinnati or Atlanta the next day.

The combination frequently resulted in too little sleep and too much caffeine. But such trips had become routine – until that Sunday in 1994 when I called home after the game at old Fulton-County Stadium.

Home is Clinton, La., a town of about 1,500 people, 30 or so miles north of Baton Rouge. I haven't lived there since 1974. It's still home, though, as you will understand if you keep reading.

It's where I grew up, went to school from kindergarten through high school, and where I made friends that have lasted a lifetime.

And it's where I have kept returning, no matter where my career has taken me.

My best trips home came when I was leaving the Army – for little more than an overnight stay while in training at Fort Polk, La., or for a week's leave when I could race home from Fort Riley, Kan., to Clinton in 15 ½ hours, sometimes driving all through the night without sleep.

I once fell asleep driving through Oklahoma City, and woke up just in time to make a sharp turn on an I-35 exit ramp. Of course, it was foolish and dangerous. But every minute at home was precious when I was stranded on a military base.

Driving long distances seemed normal to me, even before I became a sports columnist or was drafted into the Army. My friend, Mike Felps, suggested that it might be genetic.

When I informed him of a four-week trip West my wife, Melinda, and I planned to take one summer, Mike said, "That's a lot of fence posts."

He admitted there was no force pushing him to move long distances in a short time. He grew up in Clinton and never left.

"I don't have that travel gene," he said.

Apparently, I did. Moody Adams, my father, was a traveling salesman for National Biscuit Company. He drove throughout Louisiana and Mississippi long before interstates and sometimes on gravel roads. My brother, Moody Jr., estimated that dad probably drove 1,000 miles a week. And he did it for decades, until he died in January 1950 when I was only 2-1/2 years old.

My brother and I were basically "only children," born more than 17 years apart to Moody and Marie Adams, who had no other children in between.

Moody Jr. had the travel gene, too. He became an evangelist when he was only 19, after being saved at a Billy Graham crusade in Jackson, Miss., shortly after father died. A counselor at the crusade instructed him to share his conversion with someone.

He did that the next day and almost every day afterward for decades. His ministry would take him all over the world. At first, he traveled only by car, determined to meet every request for a meeting, regardless of the travel schedule that it would demand.

He left a meeting in Sacramento, Calif., and drove more than 40 hours to another meeting in the Florida Panhandle. While passing through the Mojave Desert, he saw sand dunes in the middle of the road and horses atop fence posts.

When he told me the story many years later, I felt better about my own travel. I fought through drowsiness but never, even in those hurried escapes from Ft. Riley, did I hallucinate while driving.

My mother didn't have the travel gene. She stayed at home, waiting on her husband to return for the weekend and later for her youngest son to return from wherever I was.

She was why I was going home that Sunday in 1994.

When I called her from my hotel room in Atlanta on Sunday evening, I knew right away something was terribly wrong. The person who had usually made more sense than anyone in my life suddenly was making no sense at all. A woman who had taught English and worked as a librarian - a woman who had a way with words - uttered words that had no connection to the ones that preceded them.

I left for home immediately.

Mother recovered from the initial stroke, but she no longer could live at home. She entered a nursing home in Baton Rouge near my brother's house.

Two and a half years later, I received another call to go home. My mother's kidneys had failed. Doctors said she wouldn't live more than six days.

A day I had dreaded since my earliest memories was near.

I was only eight years old when I had the worst nightmare of my life. I was walking with my mother, hand in hand, through our backyard as if in a movie, our backs to the camera. As we turned toward one another, I looked into the face of a stranger, not my mother's.

All dreams should be so easy to interpret.

Miss Margaret and I look on as my mother enjoys her retirement party at the library.

Having lost my father before my third birthday and aware that my mother was older than my friends' mothers – she had me when she was 41 – I spent my childhood fearful of losing her. The fear returned when I was in college.

I was having breakfast in Hatcher Cafeteria at LSU, when another student delivered a message from the Dean's Office. There was a family emergency I was told. Wait in front of the dorm. Someone was on the way to pick me up shortly (I wouldn't have my own car for another year, so that wasn't an option).

Obviously, something horrible had happened to my mother. Otherwise, she would have called me – perhaps to tell me there was a medical crisis involving my grandmother, who was in her 90s.

But I tried not to think about that as I waited outside my Hodges dormitory. And waited. And waited.

The ride never came.

Finally, I called the Dean's Office and found out the message had been delivered to the wrong John Adams. My mother was fine.

More than 25 years later, I was losing her again. But there was no one to call, and no one to correct an error.

Her kidneys had failed. And that's how it would end.

On the drive home, I alternately cried and consoled myself with the thought that her suffering would end soon. There was another thought, too: how grateful I was to have had her for so long. She raised me as a single mother while caring for her ageing mother at the same time. She wasn't just my mother. She was my best friend and my hero. And she was the one who said "hello" and "goodbye" when her husband left for another week on the road or when I came home from college, the military or work – only to leave again.

One of my most vivid memories is her smiling and waving goodbye from our porch as I turned around in the driveway before leaving.

There was another memory from that front porch, one that I couldn't summon on my own but was provided by my brother not that long ago.

I relied on him for stories about my father. He even went on a couple of work trips with Dad. In fact, most of his stories were about trips – from one genetically disposed traveler to another.

But one story, that I didn't hear until a few years ago, was about waiting for the traveler to come home.

After spending a year managing a store in Clinton that didn't work out, my father had returned to the road. And even as a 2-year-old, I had figured out the most important part of my dad's itinerary.

He would come home on Friday afternoon, and I would be there on the front porch to meet him.

Father was only 45 when he stopped coming home.

He had died of a heart attack. I can only guess that everyone around me – my mother, what few relatives we had and our friends – were grieving his loss while trying to assure me everything was fine, even though someone so familiar and important to my world was no longer in it.

Two-year-olds can't relate to that. So, each Friday afternoon, I would still go to the front porch. And wait for dad to come home.

My brother – not my mother - told me that story many years later. It would have been too painful for her.

I don't know how long it took me to stop waiting and realize that Fridays had become just another day. Or to become old enough to understand who was missing and why.

My world had been shaken. Processing that would take time.

I have no memory of anything before I was 5 years old. My first memory was of being afraid and not knowing why. Mother told me later she sensed I was struggling with the loss. Sometimes, for no apparent reason, I would stare into space, and my lower lip would quiver.

But I had my mother. I also had a neighborhood that became an extended family and an entire town that made me feel welcome.

I didn't just acquire friends. I acquired the friendship of their families.

There was Chuck Charlet. But there were also his parents, C.A. and Shine. Once I became friends with Phil Graham, I became friends with his parents, Buddy and Puni. Mike Felps came with his father, Sonny, and mother, Mildred.

I felt almost as comfortable in their homes as I did my own. Not just their homes, but their businesses. The Grahams had the hardware store. And the McKnights had a department store.

I went to school grades one through 12 with Louis McKnight. But I felt close to anybody who worked in that store. And that included two McKnight families.

McKnight's Department Store, located in the middle of Main Street, served as a gathering place for the entire town. You could set your watch by who was drinking coffee in the back. My mother stopped there regularly in the late afternoon after her work as a librarian was done. So, it seemed, did almost everyone else from opening to closing time.

Louis' parents, Mr. Louis (Skeet) and Miss Peggy, have died. So have Big Ikey and Marquita. What we call "downtown Clinton" isn't the same without them. But in my mind's eye, they're still there. Just like all the other businesses and families that were so important in my childhood.

I grew up without a father. I didn't have a big family. But I had a support system as big as the town.

My support system began with the McConnell family, across the street and two houses down.

My second family consisted of Mitchell and Margaret McConnell. They had three sons – Mitchell Jr., Johnny and Bobby. Mitchell was older, but I grew up around Bobby, who was two years older than me; and Johnny, four years older. Growing up, I probably never went more than two days without visiting them.

I took a second family for granted at the time. Just like I took my hometown for granted. Why wouldn't I? I didn't know anything else.

Now, I realize how lucky I was to have grown up where I did, when I did.

Saddle Up, 'Cowboy'

I called him "Big Mitch." He called me "Cowboy."

The nicknames were half-right. Mitchell McConnell surely was a big man, about 6-foot-3. But to a child, he was much taller. And as the patriarch of the McConnell Family – my second family – he was the biggest man I knew.

So "Big Mitch" was appropriate. But "Cowboy" was a stretch.

I earned the nickname by wandering around the house and yard in a cowboy hat with a pair of toy six-shooters holstered on my hips. I was pretending to be a cowboy as a 3-year-old before we had a television set, which opened my world to the likes of Roy Rogers, Gene Autry, Wild Bill Elliott, Lash Larue, and Whip Wilson – to name a few. Like me, they were all "pretend cowboys." Unlike me, they got paid to pursue their fantasies.

I outgrew my fondness for cowboy hats, but Big Mitch never stopped calling me Cowboy.

My fantasy didn't hold up well in the real world. I realized that on my first vacation. The trip was planned by my Uncle Clayton, who actually owned horses, and his wife, Gladys. They didn't have children, but were nice enough to take me and three of my cousins to Big Bend National Park, which was a long way from anywhere in Texas.

It was a great place for cowboys. But not such a great place for an 8-year-old who pretended to be a cowboy.

This cowboy had never been away from home, which meant he had never experienced homesickness. That changed on my first night on the road. Keep in mind, I had spent very little time with my aunt and uncle or any of my cousins. I remember missing my mother terribly and thinking, "If only I were with the McConnells on vacation, then I would be able to sleep and eat" (no, I didn't eat much on the trip, either, because I was nauseated the entire time).

All I remember about Big Bend National Park was the cowboy part. We were all going on a trail ride. Well, almost all of us. As we were introduced to our horses, one of my cousins started screaming and crying. She was merely vocalizing what I was thinking. But cowboys don't cry or scream, especially in the presence of their horses. So I suffered in silence while my screaming, crying cousin was fostering so much sympathy that it became perfectly acceptable for her to not take part in the horse ride up a mountain.

I was assigned a dapple-gray horse, which looked large enough to carry four 8-year-olds up and down the trail. Oddly enough, I became more comfortable as we began moving. Perhaps, it was because, even though I never had been on a horse, I sensed how slow moving this animal was. In the face of a tsunami, he would have sauntered. Still, I was relieved when the ride had ended, my cowboy image still intact.

But the happiest moment of the trip came several days later when it ended in my driveway. I hurriedly thanked my aunt and uncle for the trip and raced inside, where two ham sandwiches were waiting.

Later that evening, I was at the McConnells, telling my second family about the trip out West. My description of the horse drama was condensed into: "I rode up and down a mountain on a large horse." No problem.

But they probably knew better. In fact, I was a little surprised Bobby didn't challenge my account by asking, "How scared were you?"

Bobby and I spent a lot of time together. We played almost everything - football, basketball, baseball, golf, tennis, badminton, Ping-Pong, and croquet.

Johnny introduced me to pets. He never had a snake, but almost everything else. Animals seemed to like Johnny as much as he liked them. Mom's cocker spaniel, Tuffy, viewed the McConnell's as more than a second family, mainly because of Johnny. In Tuffy's final days, she was probably closer to Johnny than mother. If that bothered mother, she never said. I just remember her crying when Tuffy died.

Bobby's interests were more varied than Johnny's, though not as longstanding as his brother's devotion to animals. But once Bobby was interested in something, he became immersed in it until something else got his attention.

He and Dickie Barnett, who grew up a block away, spent part of a summer trying to restore a broken-down old car in the McConnell's backyard. Bobby was so excited about the project, you would have thought that eventually the car would be fit for the Daytona 500.

It never ran.

But that's not the point. The point is how much enjoyment Bobby derived from it.

Music held his interest longer than the car. And while I had no interest in what was under the hood of a car that never uttered a sound, I benefited from Bobby's enthusiasm for music. He could listen to blues, jazz or rock 'n' roll, and was more enthralled with Dave Brubek than Elvis. I didn't share his eclectic tastes, but I'm grateful he introduced me to Bob Dylan. And I'm grateful he had a stereo since all I had in my early teen years was a huge radio console. The bottom compartment had a Victrola, whose turntable was capable of playing 45 records.

When I was 15, I went to Baton Rouge with the McConnells to see the movie "Bye, Bye Birdie" at the Paramount Theater. The movie began and ended with a young Ann-Margret, wearing a beige blouse and skirt, singing the title song on an otherwise empty stage. She was clearly the most beautiful woman I had ever seen. I was so impressed that I bought the movie's record album in the lobby as soon as the movie ended – even though I couldn't play it at home.

But that wasn't necessary. I had the McConnells.

For a while, golf was Bobby's primary interest. So I picked it up, too. Bobby was good at it, and – on my best days – I could manage not to lose a bag full of golf balls.

I don't remember great shots or good rounds so much as I remember things going wrong. Even when I was in my late 50s, before I gave up the sport for the last time, my strongest memories of golf were Bobby and I getting caught in a thunderstorm on the farthest side of a Denham Springs course, and a nightmarish round on the Mississippi Gulf Coast that ended on the fourth hole with both of our bags covered in mosquitoes.

Based on my introduction to golf, I should have anticipated such mishaps.

When Bobby and I arrived at Sharon Meadows Golf Course, eight miles outside of Clinton, for my official introduction to the sport, I believed I was appropriately dressed for the occasion: a baseball cap, t-shirt, swimming trunks, and baseball spikes. Bobby didn't say anything about the cleats. Nor did he mention what I was doing to the greens, which weren't what you would call "manicured," but at least weren't defaced with cleat marks until I launched my golfing career.

When we reached the clubhouse after 18 holes, owner O.J. Lea looked at me with horror. "Are you playing in those?" he asked.

I pleaded ignorance, which was an honest assessment. Bobby just laughed. He probably had been imagining that look on O.J.'s face for 18 holes.

Something else stuck with me from playing golf with Bobby. Anytime someone hits a long tee shot into the middle of a fairway, I remember how he would loudly characterize his own best drives within seconds of making contact: "I knocked the pee-wine snot out of that one."

High praise, and uttered with such confidence that I never felt compelled to compliment Bobby's shots. Even if I had thought praise was appropriate, he would have beaten me to it.

Bobby didn't withhold compliments from his younger, less experienced partner. If I managed to hit the ball straight and a decent distance, I could count on him saying, "That's a nice lady-like tap, John Dean." I settled for that, realizing not even

I can't imagine what my childhood would have been like without Miss Margaret and Big Mitch.

my best drives would be honored with, "You knocked the pee-wine snot out of that one." Come to think of it, I can't remember Bobby saying that about anyone else's drive, either. It was a Bobby-only compliment.

Big Mitch never helped me with my golf game. But he helped me with almost everything else.

When mother bought me a bike, I was uncertain whether I could ride it. Big Mitch quickly came to my assistance. "Cowboy, let's go up to the football field," he said. And off we went.

He put me on the bike, which he held steady, then told me to pedal and keep my balance as I pedaled. A biker was born.

And thanks again to Big Mitch, I became a race-car driver. Actually, it was a soap-box derby, which required that the drivers help build the racer – with the help of their father. Big Mitch substituted as my father, of course. And he did most of the building while I held things, watched, and painted.

The combination worked beautifully, and I finished third. If I hadn't been slowed by a huge bump on the right side of Bank Street's downhill slope, I'm convinced I would have won.

Big Mitch also took me as close as I would ever get to ranching.

The "Place" was Big Mitch's home away from home. A few miles outside Clinton, you turned left off the Greensburg Highway on to a gravel road, which later turned into a dirt road. There was a barn and pond. But mostly, there were cattle. Managing the cattle was Big Mitch's hobby.

For rather sedentary animals, they weren't always that easy to manage, especially when the managing was partially dependent on Big Mitch's helpers – Johnny, Bobby, and me.

The cows did fine when little was required of them. You could count on them to stand in place, swat flies, and walk in file to a feed trough. But ask them to expand their repertoire and they balked, like when we had to worm them.

The process didn't go smoothly. I felt out of my element, but also noticed that neither Bobby nor Johnny distinguished themselves, which meant Big Mitch had to scream a lot whenever he sensed the task was on the brink of failure.

Big Mitch never cursed. He invented words, which I can't spell, that he shouted with great conviction and always succeeded in getting our attention. He also had an ability to turn very red while shouting.

But even in my darkest hour as a cattleman, he still called me "Cowboy" afterward.

Big Mitch was my ranch foreman, carpenter, builder, and driving instructor. Miss Margaret was my art director. She could make anything and was unfailingly creative, no matter what the assignment. Anytime my assignment required a poster I could rely on Miss Margaret's assistance.

Not only was she creative and artistic, she could relate to children of any age better than any adult I've ever known. It's no wonder she made such an exceptional sixth-grade teacher.

She also had a child-like exuberance for life. You could see that in how she decorated her house for Christmas. In fact, she made every holiday special.

In the days leading up to my 10th Christmas, I began receiving clues from Miss Margaret. The last one was a Benadryl, which suggested my gift would be so stunning, I would require sedation.

The buildup continued when I opened the gift, which was a box that contained a smaller box, and then an even smaller one. As I tore through a succession of boxes, I was left with an envelope.

In it was a Sugar Bowl ticket for LSU vs. Clemson. LSU's unbeaten team needed a victory over Clemson in the Sugar Bowl to finish No. 1 in the polls and claim the 1958 national championship in college football.

And thanks to the McConnell's family connections, we would be seated on the 45-yard line. They had gotten the tickets from Clemson coach Frank Howard, who was a relative of theirs.

That's not the only time I benefited from the McConnell's extended family. Miss Margaret's sister, Sarah, lived in Houston. One summer, Miss Margaret took me with her when she went to visit her sister.

It was my first train ride. Better than that, it gave me a chance to watch my favorite baseball team, the Pittsburgh Pirates, play Houston in old Colt .45 Stadium.

Miss Sarah's son Terry took me to the game. I repaid him by leaping as high as I could to catch a foul ball of the bat of my favorite player, Roberto Clemente. My desperate reach for the ball blocked the view of Terry, who was seated behind me.

I couldn't catch the ball, but the ball caught Terry, striking him just above the right eye. Ice healed the wound, and he wasn't even angry at me for blinding him to the oncoming baseball.

After all, I was family.

Crossing Plank Road

My neighborhood had plenty going for it, but let's start with the obvious: location.

The school was just a block to the south. Downtown was little more than a block away to the north. So was the Methodist church, which Mike Felps and I joined during the same service at the age of 8.

Playmates were even closer than my church and school.

John Irwin Stewart was about 500 yards away, just east of Plank Road. We were the same age and close friends in our preteen years. Since it was appropriate to call people by two names in those days, John Dean and John Irwin were easily confused. Even now, when I return to Clinton, I'm still occasionally called "John Irwin" without the offending party ever noticing the mistake.

The Bennetts, William and Mary, lived next door to the south with their three children – Lettie, Melanie and Bill. And the McConnells were just down the street.

I never heard, "Don't get too close to your neighbors." That didn't apply when and where I grew up. Part of my neighborhood was like family, but not the kind of family you dread having to waste a holiday with. In fact, I even had real relatives in the neighborhood.

Miss Sue Record, Mother's first cousin, lived across the street from the Bennetts with her mother Mamie Record and her sister Annie Mae. Miss Mamie and Annie Mae both died when I was young. Miss Sue lived to be 100, and even in her late 90s was still doing yard work.

At the southern end of what I considered my neighborhood was Polk's Auto, managed by Hubert and Ruby Polk. They met in North Louisiana, got married, and moved to Jackson, where Mr. Hubert went to work as a mechanic before they opened their Texaco Station and repair shop on Plank Road.

Mr. Hubert was an inventor and could fix just about anything with an engine in it. Miss Ruby managed the front portion of the shop. Even though she was pretty and well dressed, she still pumped gas at their full-service station. She also was a great conversationalist, so I didn't need gas for our lawnmower for an excuse to visit.

Their contributions to the neighborhood included more than gas and auto repairs. One of Miss Ruby's sisters had a camp on False River, and the Polks later bought a fishing camp of their own at Lake Rosemond. It wasn't uncommon for Miss Ruby to stop by our house with fried perch or with tomatoes and peas from the large garden Mr. Hubert tended on one side of their house.

I also saw my first television show at the Polk's house. They invited a group of us too watch "The $64,000 Question."

Next to the Polk's service station was the home of Landry and Katherine Richardson, who had two daughters, Julia and Sue. Mr. Landry owned land with cattle across from the McConnell's place. The cattle were his hobby, too.

Mr. Landry and Big Mitch got out of the service about the same time, and the 100-acre tract of land not far from the Greensburg Highway was for sale. Neither one had the money to buy the entire lot. But they pooled their money, bought the land, and split it equally.

The Richardsons, Polks, Bennetts, McConnells and Miss Sue comprised the heart of my neighborhood. While there was turnover elsewhere in the neighborhood, they were always there growing up. I valued their friendship and consistency.

A perfect world? Almost.

But there were obstacles. For example, the stand of trees between our house and the Bennetts was a haven for mosquitoes in the summer. So was the uncovered drainage ditch that ran by the side of our house.

Sometimes, I thought the mosquitoes picked on me. But they clearly favored Lettie, who had the fairest skin in the neighborhood.

While I enjoyed being around her throughout childhood, I especially valued her friendship in the summer when the mosquitoes were out. As the mosquitoes' second-favorite choice, it was a relief to have their favorite choice nearby. The ditch was an annoyance in that a poorly thrown baseball could wind up in it.

Later, I wondered if there were greater negatives to having grown up next to a drainage ditch.

When I was six years old, I contracted what was diagnosed as a mild case of polio. I don't remember being in pain or even discomfort, but I had what amounted to a crick in my neck for almost an entire summer when I was 6. My cowboy hat just didn't look the same with my head tilted decidedly to the right. But the strange symptom, like the whelps from mosquito bites, eventually cleared up.

The greatest challenge of our neighborhood stretched out in front of us from the Main Street intersection all the way to Baton Rouge. On the map, it was Highway 67. But everybody called it Plank Road. It had a deadly history.

Most of that history centered around a wicked curve between Miss Sue's and the Bennett's, before straightening out in front of our house. My brother said there was more than one fatal wreck in the curve. Many of the wrecks were from north-bound traffic.

Before the curve, there was a huge hill leading into town. Cars coming from Baton Rouge on the way to somewhere in Mississippi would pick up speed going down the hill before they encountered the sudden, sharp turn.

Moody Jr. was in the living room with Mother one night when they heard an awful crash. When they went outside, they saw an overturned car and heard a man screaming. He was bloodied, and skin was peeled off his arms. But he was alive.

Convinced that the driver was going too fast to make the turn, the front-seat passenger gambled that his chances would be better if he jumped from than car. He was right.

Not everyone was that fortunate.

Two Zachary High School students were killed in one crash. They had attended a dance at the American Legion Hall and apparently were headed south back to Zachary.

They ran into trouble before the curve, though.

As they tried to turn right on Plank Road from Main Street, the car went out of control, veering up the embankment of the Kline's house. The car came off the embankment onto the road. But witnesses said it picked up speed and crashed in the curve. A third passenger lived after being ejected from the car.

Not all the wayward cars crashed. Some just plowed through our driveway. That happened so often that father went on the defensive. He took a pair of coupling poles off a truck, fastened them into the ground and filled the holes with concrete.

He thought the problem had been solved. And it was – until the next car lost control in the curve.

"It snapped off the poles like matchsticks," my brother said.

Growing up in the neighborhood, we learned the peril of forgetting the paved danger not far from our doorstep. My closest call came just after I was old enough to cross Plank Road without an accompanying adult. I was halfway into the second lane when a car came around the curve. I looked right at the driver, who was more scared than I was when she hit her brakes as hard as she could.

Driving onto the road was as dangerous as crossing it on foot. As a 15-year-old with a new driver's license, parallel parking wasn't nearly as challenging as backing up southward onto Plank Road before swiftly shifting into drive and heading for downtown.

We became so honed in on Plank Road traffic that we could hear trouble coming. Once, when Bill, Melanie, and I were playing baseball in our backyard, we almost simultaneously sensed a crash was coming. We could tell by the sound that the car was going too fast to make the turn.

We abandoned our game and raced to the front yard, just in time to see a plumber's truck overturned in the ditch to the right of our driveway. The plumber was OK, but nuts and bolts were scattered throughout the ditch.

Perhaps, we benefited from the threat that Plank Road posed. Maybe, it made us more careful drivers, or heightened our awareness to the suddenness with which things can change.

Ultimately, we got the best of Plank Road. We didn't let it restrict our movements within the neighborhood. But we made sure to move carefully.

Gratefully, Plank Road wasn't widened to four lanes until after we were grown.

Four lanes didn't decrease the size of the hill leading into town. Nor did they straighten the curve in front of my house. Now, you have to cross four lanes instead of two. And you have to do so in the face of faster traffic.

The traffic was fast enough when we were growing up. Our pets faced the same challenge that we did.

Because of Johnny's attraction to almost any living creature, the McConnells had more animals than anyone, some of whom didn't have to cross Plank Road.

One of Johnny's pets was an exotic finch, whose home was a cage on the front porch. Once, when I opened the screen door, I noticed the finch was no longer there.

Miss Margaret told me it had escaped the cage and flown away. That seemed odd at the time, and even odder years later when I concluded the finch had died in its cage. But a bird flying off into freedom makes a better children's story than a bird dying in its cage.

Annie Mae always had several cats. Mary Norwood might have had more cats than anyone in town, and most of them had six toes. The Bennett's had a wonderful dog named Poochie. She should have been named "Friendly." Everybody liked Poochie except for my Siamese cat, Lenny.

Mother never got another dog after Tuffy died. But she got me a series of cats, not all of whom survived Plank Road.

My first cat, Calico, was black and white and fierce. Mother once saw her kill a squirrel on the back lot. She caught it from behind and strangled it. I watched her fighting a nonpoisonous snake near the drainage ditch. Calico lost interest before the battle was decided.

I'm not sure what happened to Calico. She just disappeared one day.

All I remember about my next cat was that she was white and didn't live long enough for me to decide on a name. She died on Plank Road.

After the unnamed white cat, I had Roberto, a Tabby that was named after baseball player Roberto Clemente. He lasted a few years before wandering off like Calico.

Lenny, who was named after Baltimore Colts running back Lenny Moore, was nothing like any of the other pets. Mother got her as my Christmas present when I was 16. Lenny lasted longer than all our other pets combined, finally dying of old age at 18, long after I had left home.

Lenny was an extraordinary cat, capable of jumping from the floor to the mantle in the living room. She preferred jumping on top of the television set in the den. From that vantage point, she would stare at us or look down at the screen, where a weatherman's pointer got her attention more than once.

So did the Rolling Stones in what was one of their first national television appearances. As Mick Jagger twisted, twitched, and jumped on stage, Lenny pawed at the screen from above.

The television didn't quench her sense of adventure. She loved to climb trees. And no tree, including the biggest oak in our yard, was too tall. Unlike some cats, she had no fear of descent. Although her high climbs scared Mother and me, they didn't faze Lenny. She would

Lenny preferred sitting on the television to watching it.

climb close to the top, perch a while, then come down without hesitation whenever she chose.

Her sense of boundaries was her most remarkable attribute. She didn't wander into the Bennett's yard or venture beyond our back lot. More importantly, she never attempted to cross the road out front. She would walk down the sidewalk that led from our front doorstep, stop a few feet from the end, and watch the traffic go by.

She understood Plank Road better than anyone.

Introducing the Pittsburgh Pirates

Everyone in our neighborhood, pets included, needed to be aware of the danger that Plank Road posed. But that didn't mean we felt unsafe. In fact, I couldn't have imagined a safer neighborhood. Or a more helpful one.

While the McConnells became my official second family, I also wondered if the entire neighborhood had been assembled for my benefit.

Miss Margaret taught sixth grade. Miss Sue taught high school English, typing, and served as Clinton High's librarian for many years. Both helped me along my career path.

Miss Margaret didn't just teach what was in a book. She brought the subjects to life, often through her own travels. She encouraged creativity and challenged you to look beyond a small-town classroom.

She taught us to sing a German song. And it left an impression. More than 50 years later, when it came up in conversation, Ginger Pullig and I started singing it at the same time.

Miss Margaret also required students with no sense of art to paint her a picture with crayons. The art assignment challenged me since my drawing skill was limited to stick figures. But I did my best. My best: two grassy mounds with a single tree on each, fronted by a pool of water.

I fared better on another assignment: "What do you want to be when you grow up?"

That's when I realized I wanted to be a writer. More specifically, I wanted to write about sports.

I responded to the assignment by writing an account of the Clinton Eagles' most recent game.

My lead: "The Clinton Eagles overcame fumbles and penalties to beat Kentwood 26-6 in Clinton Friday night."

Catchy, huh?

I might have been the only student in the class who, at 12 years old, knew how he wanted to earn a living. But I bet everyone in Miss Margaret's class at least considered their possibilities.

I didn't take a formal course under Miss Sue. But she taught me how to type when I was 15. That was significant, because a few months later, Roland and Malva Huson hired me to write weekly accounts of Clinton's football games.

Miss Sue didn't teach me the way she taught her students. She showed me how to position my fingers on the Underwood Standard typewriter, gave me a typing textbook, and told me to take speed tests. That was it.

Initially, I missed as many keys as I hit. But I kept hitting away at full speed. By the end of the summer, I could average 75 words per minute with only a few mistakes.

I was ready to begin my sports writing career.

Not all my writings were published. I would watch a game on television or listen to one on the radio, then – imagining I was on deadline – furiously type away on the Underwood.

Miss Margaret and Miss Sue weren't the only teachers in the neighborhood. Miss Thelma Knighten, who lived behind the Bennett's house, and Miss Lewis McKneely, who lived behind our house and one lot over, also were teachers. Mary Norwood, who lived next door to Miss Sue, tutored students – all of whom she treated to punch and cookies.

"Momma sent me to her because she wanted me to read better," Billy Joe Yarbrough said. "She was a little biddy lady in a little biddy house. You could hardly walk in there it was so crowded."

Miss Mary, whom the children in our neighborhood called Mae Mae could have had more room. She owned a bigger house that fronted on Plank Road. But she chose to rent that house and live in the cottage behind it.

Mae Mae's cats had no problem with the crowded accommodations. They ran wild throughout the house. On one of my visits, I counted more than 10. But they were moving so fast, maybe I saw five or six cats twice in a matter of seconds.

"When I would walk in, some of them looked like they wanted to eat you," Billy said. "There was a big yellow cat that was always in the front room. He just glared at me."

For a while, there was a dentist across the street, and an elementary school principal, Jim Soileau, next door. When I was in high school, the Lagroues – Lula and her two daughters Genevieve and Catherine - moved into the house across the street. Mrs. Lagroue became the first fulltime pharmacist at the infirmary. Until then, doctors had filled their own prescriptions.

The house to the north of the Lagroues had been in the Freeland family since the 1800s. Emile Freeland was never there when I was growing up, though. He was too busy traveling the world as a chemical engineer.

Sugar chemists often were referred to as "sugar tramps," which explained the title of his book, "Tales of a Sugar Tramp."

At the age of 71, he fulfilled a lifelong goal by enrolling at Oxford University in England. At the time, he was the oldest student ever admitted to the prestigious university.

My grandmother and mother were librarians. Big Mitch worked at the Soil Conservation Service office and did surveying on the side. William Bennett was a lawyer and then a judge. He also was a patriot and a paratrooper.

After Pearl Harbor was bombed, he was determined to fight for his country. He needed the persuasive powers of an attorney to get in. He convinced Dr. Clovis Toler to verify in writing that he had a sound heart when, in fact, he had an irregular heartbeat. He also sold the military on not holding his age against him.

And at 39, the former R.O.T.C. cadet joined the Army. He underwent training in the U.S. and in England, where he learned to be a glider pilot. After the war, he would be stationed in both Japan and Korea, where he rose to the rank of colonel.

The Bennetts pose in front of their antebellum home for a Christmas card. Judge William Bennett is flanked by his daughter, Melanie, and his son Bill. Below are Miss Mary and daughter, Lettie.

You could see antiques from where he was stationed if you toured the Bennett's antebellum home. And people toured it regularly. But I got in for free.

I didn't fully appreciate the beauty of their house as a kid, but my mother did. When I was at LSU, I used it as a directional landmark for college friends coming up from Baton Rouge.

"Just as you get into town on Plank Road and right in the hairpin curve, you will see an antebellum home with large, white columns, and manicured hedges out front," I would begin.

As their interest perked up, I would pause before adding … "Well, my house is the next one on the left."

Although I was in their house often, I never experienced anything unusual. But the Bennett children did. They never told me any ghost stories until we were adults. Maybe, they didn't want to scare me away.

"There were several unexplained experiences," Lettie said. "Melanie has her stories. I have mine."

Lettie remembers lying on a sofa in the back parlor when she heard someone calling her name. She was so certain that she walked throughout the house, including the upstairs. No one was there.

Lettie's best story was secondhand, after Buddy and Carol Shirley purchased the house.

One of the workers who was helping the Shirleys refurbish the house brought a "yappity dog" with him. Carol told Lettie that while the dog was barking away, the worker kept dropping his tools. He would pick them up, then drop them again. He was spooked enough to leave the job.

"Melanie and I laughed about it," Lettie said. "Daddy didn't like yappity dogs. We felt like daddy's presence was there, and he wanted that dog out of there."

Melanie said she sometimes would "catch something out of the corner of my eye" as though an uninvited guest were present.

"I never felt frightened by any of it," she said. "It wasn't like I thought somebody was going to get me."

Although I was oblivious to those ghost stories as a kid, I thought our neighborhood was interesting enough as it was.

I never had much trouble conversing with adults. I think that was because of the adults in my neighborhood. They were interesting people.

So were the children.

Even at 12, Lettie seemed like an adult. A voracious reader, she kept a dictionary at her side when reading and looked up every word she didn't know. She probably had a bigger vocabulary than anyone in Clinton. Not surprisingly, she became a librarian.

Bill, who was the youngest of the Bennett children, was more at home with a bicycle than a book. It was as though he learned to walk one day, then learned to ride a bike the next day. And it seemed he never stopped riding.

The only time he fell off was by design. He would mount the bike in his backyard and pick up speed on the downhill slope that went through our backyard. He would be going full speed when he leaped off the bike, just before it ran into the drainage ditch.

Bill also joined Melanie, Bobby McConnell, and me in more conventional sports, all of which could be played in my backyard or on our back lot, which extended to a street far behind the house, a block away from Plank Road.

Since Bill preferred to be on the move, the baseball games could be frustrating. He would scream his displeasure as I went through the pregame ritual of introducing the starting lineup of the 1960s Pittsburgh Pirates.

I would run to the bush that served as third base and pretend to be Don Hoak, then to the second base bush and announce Bill Mazeroski to the make-believe crowd. I went through the entire lineup while Bill – weary of waiting for the first pitch - pounded his bat on the home-plate ground and shouted, "Throw the ball."

As irritating as those pregame introductions might have been, Bill and Melanie were excited as I was when I unwrapped a package with a Pirates logo prominently displayed on the envelope. It was a plastic Pirates batting helmet, which I subsequently wore for all neighborhood sporting events.

Bill was so impressed that he bought me the next Roberto Clemente bat he saw. How many kids are that thoughtful?

Not everyone in the neighborhood would have impulsively bought a baseball bat for a hitter as bad as I was. But I always had the feeling everybody in the neighborhood cared about everybody else in the neighborhood. I know they cared about Annie Mae, who sadly died of a heart attack in her early 40s.

She was mentally handicapped. But I didn't think of her as being handicapped. I didn't think of her as being unhappy, either.

I have a large framed photo above my mantle of the home across the street, where Annie Mae and Miss Sue lived their entire lives.

Annie Mae, who was just a child, is standing in the front yard, looking perfectly content. Why wouldn't she? She had her pet cats. She also had a loving mother and sister to look after her.

And she had our neighborhood.

Hold Your Breath

Most people feel fortunate to have one memorable neighborhood. I had two.

The one that fronted on Plank Road was No. 1. But my No. 2 neighborhood was just a short bike ride away on Bank Street.

I also took the longer route, because there were few better downhill slopes than going north on Bank Street. When I hit level ground, I was almost at Phil Graham's house. That was a regular Saturday morning stop in the fall when I was 12 years old.

Phil's front lawn was our football field. And our opponents were always the same - Jimmy Morris and Billy Percy. Based on age, this matchup should have been a mismatch. Jimmy was 11, and Billy was only 9.

Phil and I usually won but often by the narrowest of margins. Our advantage didn't seem to matter when Billy had the ball. He was short, stocky, and extremely strong for his age and size.

Tackling him took the best combined effort of Phil and me. Even that often wasn't enough. Sometimes, I felt as though Billy could have carried Phil, me, and his own teammate across our makeshift goal line.

Billy was naturally strong and had hardened himself to the game of football before he was old enough to appreciate the sport. Phil told me before we played our first game that at a very young age, Billy enjoyed butting heads with a pet goat. He enjoyed it so much that his parents finally ordered him to use a helmet.

The story served a purpose, letting me know that even though Billy was only 9, playing a contact sport with someone who regularly butted heads with a goat would not be easy.

My Bank Street buddies, Chuck Charlet (left) and Phil Graham.

The Charlet Funeral Home was at the other end of Bank Street. C.A. and Shine Charlet lived in an adjoining area of the funeral home. That's where Chuck grew up. And that's where Chuck and I played extremely long basketball games.

The games took so long because of our scoring system.

If people had passed by while a game was in progress, they would have seen two kids playing one-on-one. But it was much more complicated than that. In fact, we were both representing NBA teams. I was the St. Louis Hawks, and Chuck was the Boston Celtics.

We kept a pen and piece of paper beside the court for scoring purposes. If Chuck posted me up and scored close to the basket, the points would be logged under the name of Celtics center Bill Russell. If I made a shot from the baseline, the points usually were credited to the Hawks' Bob Pettit. If I hit a hook shot, Cliff Hagan got the points.

Sounds like too much work, doesn't it? But we didn't mind.

I became familiar with other houses on Bank Street during my childhood.

John and Yetta Rogers didn't live far from the funeral home. He was a former Clinton High principal, and she was a longtime school teacher.

I remember spending several Saturday afternoons there one March. I would watch college basketball games with Mr. Rogers while scarfing down the tea cookies Miss Yetta made.

We watched the games in Mr. Rogers' bedroom, because his body wouldn't let him go much farther than that. We could relate to each other as two basketball fans, but there was an undercurrent of discomfort for me.

The last time I saw him, I thought we wouldn't share many more basketball games together. But I tried not to think about that as I ate Miss Yetta's tea cookies, and Mr. Rogers and I watched the Louisville-Cincinnati game.

The next morning at church, I overheard just enough of an adult conversation to know that Mr. Rogers had died the night before. I felt an awful sinking feeling. And even though I knew he had been bedridden for a while and seemed less engaged than usual on my last visit, I was still surprised.

I realized I might have been the last person to visit him. I felt sadness, not just about his dying but that I hadn't known him better.

Miss Yetta was regarded as one of our most demanding teachers, whether the subject was history, English or French. If you entered her class unprepared, you ran the risk of being terribly embarrassed.

When I took two years of French under her, I probably got off easy. But I couldn't take satisfaction from that. I just remembered that sinking feeling from years earlier.

Alice Chambers, who also lived on Bank Street, remembered a tougher Miss Yetta.

"I was a little afraid of her," Alice said. "She told me if I won district and state at literary rally, I wouldn't have to do any more history for the rest of the year."

Alice did just that.

"She didn't think I was going to win," Alice said. "But she

had to abide by it."

Alice's house became a gathering place during our junior and senior years of high school. The pool table was an attraction.

The house I remembered was the Chambers' second house on Bank Street. The first one burned down when Alice's cousin, who was staying with them, left her nylon panties hanging above a heater to dry. That night, they fell onto the heater and caught the house on fire.

I knew Alice's mother, Miss Opal, from the hospital. I didn't know much about her father, McWillie, till later.

I'm sure he could have beaten any of us at pool. He also was a good swimmer, skater, and dancer. But his preferred sport involved horses.

"He was a professional rodeo rider when I was little," Alice said. "Back then, tall people didn't ride bulls. He was 6-4. But he did calf roping and steer wrestling, and rode bucking horses."

Of course, anyone who rides a bucking horse eventually gets bucked off. Alice's dad suffered a fractured skull from one fall.

Doctors sentenced him to six weeks of bed rest. He had other ideas. After all, cowboys don't call in sick, particularly when they have paid an entry fee for a rodeo.

"Daddy came downstairs all dressed up," said Alice, who was sitting on the floor. "He and Momma got into an argument. She pointed to me and said, 'You've got responsibilities now."

Her father made one concession to the demands of family life before Alice was born.

"Early in 1947, Daddy had a yellow Buick convertible," Alice said. "It was a big deal back then to have a yellow convertible.

"Momma said she told him when she got pregnant that he had to get rid of the car, because you couldn't have a baby in a convertible," Alice said.

Confronted with making a choice between a baby and a convertible, he didn't answer right away.

"It was as though he was thinking it over," Miss Opal told Alice.

When Mr. McWillie's yellow convertible and rodeo days were behind him, he settled for driving an 18-wheeler. He also was a teamster and bought and sold cows.

It was an eclectic household. Not only did you have a nurse and a cowboy, McWillie Jr. was already demonstrating artistic skills and later would become a famous New York artist. Alice's high intellect also was apparent early on.

"I started reading books when I was about 4," Alice said. "My grandmother lived with us and she read to me and Mac."

It didn't take long for Alice to figure out she could read, too. Once she started reading, she never slowed down. There weren't enough books in the house to satiate her appetite. One summer, she read the World Book encyclopedia from A to Z.

When the Audubon Regional Library opened, Alice might have been the happiest person in town. In an average week during the summer, she read seven books.

"Miss Marie (my mother) asked me once, 'Are you really reading all these books?' " Alice said. "One time, I read an entire book while waiting for Momma to pick me up. So, I asked Miss Marie if I could get another book.

"She said you really weren't supposed to check out a book and check it back in the same day. But I looked so bereft, she let me."

She kept reading at a rapid rate all the way through college, which she found more stimulating than high school.

"I got in trouble in school for just being bored," Alice said. "I was a better student in college. I probably graduated with 200-something hours."

Bank Street also had its share of mayors. Phil's father, Mr. Buddy, was mayor when I was in high school. Toler Hatcher, who lived next to the Charlet Funeral Home, was mayor from 1997 to 2005.

When I was in high school, I knew Mr. Toler as the trainer for the Eagles football team. He was overqualified for the job, having been a trainer for the LSU football and boxing teams when he was in college.

Since I was the team statistician, I often rode with Mr. Toler to the away games. He was such a great storyteller that I wished our road trips had been longer.

I can't remember much about Phil's daddy being mayor, except for a holiday scam that didn't turn out well.

The week before Thanksgiving one year, Phil and I came up with an idea that wasn't exactly in the spirit of the holiday. We would pick names randomly from the thin Clinton phone book. I would switch into my best radio voice when the stranger answered the call and introduce myself as a radio disc jockey.

"Today's your lucky day," I would begin. "You've just won a Thanksgiving turkey."

I'm sure I overstated the strangers' good fortune, but they seemed genuinely excited.

And what did they have to do to win the turkey? Just call back the number I gave them, which, of course, was the Graham's residence.

When they called, Phil would answer in a tone altogether different from mine. He informed the caller that he also had been victimized. I think his exact words were something like, "They done pulled the wool over my eyes, too."

We successfully executed our plan on several victims but didn't cover our tracks well. We circled the numbers in the phone book, which might have not been crucial if one of our victims hadn't called the mayor's office to complain.

I can't remember what sentence Mr. Buddy imposed on Phil, but the incident taught me the value of details.

Phil's judgment might have not been the best, but there was nothing wrong with his work ethic. He was about 8 years old when he decided to provide the family with its Christmas tree.

The Chambers were having dinner when McWillie noticed Phil demonstrating his work ethic outside their window.

"Some boy is chopping down your tree, Opal," McWillie said.

When they noticed what was going on outside, it was too late. Thanks to Phil, the Grahams had their family Christmas tree.

My second-grade teacher, Miss Genie White, lived on the far end of Bank Street from the mayor. She was one of the nicest teachers I ever had.

One of her two sons was as likable as his mother. Sid White, who quarterbacked the Eagles to a state championship in 1950, was an assistant football coach and physical education teacher.

Coach Sid was once all set to be a college quarterback. He was starting for LSU's freshman team in 1951 when he injured his right shoulder in a scrimmage against the varsity. He transferred to Hinds Junior College and then Southwestern Louisiana. Although he played quarterback at both places, his throwing arm was never the same after that injury.

That didn't end his football career, though. In addition to winning state championship as a Clinton quarterback, he won state championships with the Eagles as an assistant coach in 1962 and as a head coach in 1968.

Coach Sid and coach Hubert Polk were longtime friends, played together and coached together, but they had a different approach to football. Unlike most coaches of that era, Coach Sid didn't mind taking chances (i.e., throwing the ball).

After falling short of the playoffs in the 1959 season, Clinton played Plaquemine in the Capitol City Bowl at Memorial Stadium in Baton Rouge. Before the game, Coach Sid told his senior quarterback, Larry Castello: "Larry this is going to be the last football game you ever play. So, just go out there and have fun."

Larry took his assistant coach's words to heart. And that was fine with his teammates.

When Coach Polk sent in a play with a substitute, Larry would send him back to the sideline and call a play of his liking. Suddenly, a team that had rarely thrown the ball all season was throwing often and effectively.

"Didn't Coach Polk say anything at halftime?" I asked Larry.

"What could he say?" Larry said. "We were winning about 28-0."

The next year, when Larry was at Southeastern Louisiana University, he met a former Plaquemine player who had been in that game.

"We would have beaten you if you hadn't thrown the ball," he said. "We didn't think y'all would throw at all."

Clinton won a state championship with Coach Polk's conservative, disciplined approach and won another state title under Coach Sid with a more wide-open offense. Both systems worked, but players seemingly had more fun playing for Coach Sid.

My brother knew Sid better than I did. They were good friends growing up. Unfortunately for my brother, he also knew Sid's older brother, Jimmy. He lived in fear of him.

As much as Sid liked football, Jimmy liked fighting. To say he was a bully didn't do him justice or properly characterize the challenges of his victims. Once, Jimmy held Moody under water so long Moody thought he was going to drown.

When I heard that story, I was grateful that I only knew Sid, not Jimmy. And I also was grateful that I didn't hang out on Bank Street 17 years earlier.

My brother could hold his breath for three minutes. I couldn't hold mine half that long.

'Let It Burn'

Clinton wasn't any more populated in the late 1950s and early 1960s than it is now. But you wouldn't guess that if you saw downtown then and now.

While Main Street often looks deserted today, it was teeming with people when I was young. The crowds were biggest on Saturday when farmers, sawmill workers, and others who resided in rural areas came into town to shop.

Downtown was so busy on Saturday that skating wasn't allowed on the sidewalk. For kids, skating was second only to bicycling when it came to downtown transportation.

Cars were parked parallel on both sides of the street, and spots were hard to come by on Saturday. There were plenty of stores to accommodate the shoppers.

Nobody should have starved, that was for sure. Grocery stories were everywhere. I can remember seven stores, and most of them were in business at the same time.

Some of the grocery stores had delivery service, so you could call in an order and get your groceries via pickup truck. They also offered charge accounts, which were good for the entire family. A kid could stop off at his favorite grocery store on the way home from school, buy snack food, and charge it to his parents' account.

If you didn't want to cook, there was Hubbs Café on one side of Main Street and Huds Café on the other side. The Malt Shop, owned by Jessie and Maggie Castello, also opened in the 1950s. That gave Clinton its first sandwich shop. The featured meal was a burger and malt.

Both Mr. Castello and his wife had other fulltime jobs, so they alternated running the malt shop. Their son Larry was involved, too.

After school, Larry headed downtown for the malt shop where he made malts and cooked burgers. Lucky for Larry and Clinton High football, you didn't practice football after school in those days. Instead, football players had all-morning classes, then practiced football in the afternoon.

The Malt Shop became a gathering place for teenagers, just as the Snack Shack did later.

"A.C. 'Sparky" Feierabend (Mr. Ikey McKnight gave him the nickname) and his wife, Mildred, owned the Snack Shack. It was their second business in Clinton. Earlier, they had a general store downtown.

For a while, the Feierabend's had the only meat market in town. When they opened the Snack Shack, hamburger steak was a big attraction.

The Snack Shack's business hours also were appealing.

"We would be open till 10 o'clock every night," the Feierabend's son, Ronnie, said. "On nights when there was a dance at the Legion Hall, we would stay open till 2. Everybody would come at intermission or after the dance.

"To me, I grew up in 'Happy Days.' I was there every day (at the Snack Shack). It was a big social place. We had a juke box, pool table, Foosball."

They also had .45 records. Lots of them.

"We had hundreds and hundreds of records," Ronnie said. "Boxes and boxes full of them. They gave them away when we closed. I wish we still had them today."

By the time the Feierabends opened the Snack Shack on the Greensburg Highway, the downtown restaurants had gone by the wayside.

Marie Hudnall sold Huds Café in the late 1950s and went to work as a deputy clerk of court for the next 20 years. No doubt, she appreciated the shorter work day. Since the restaurant served breakfast, lunch and dinner, she would be at the café by 4:30 in the morning and get home at 10 p.m. And she would cook all the desserts.

Hadley Hudnall, who was one of her three sons, found the café to be an educational experience.

"I didn't learn my numbers at Miss Lytle's (kindergarten)," Hadley said. "I learned them on our pinball machine. An eight to me was a double zero."

Hadley had a great deal going.

As Ted Chaney remembers, Hubbs Café opened even earlier. It opened early enough that his father, Clyde, would go there before he went to his dairy.

"Mr. Mac Hubbs couldn't sleep well," Ted said. "So, he probably opened for breakfast around 3 a.m. I can still see him sitting behind the counter swatting the few flies that got in there."

Clinton residents like Mr. Sonny Felps and Mr. Wellington Carter, who commuted to Baton Rouge to work at Exxon, also were a part of the early-morning crowd at Hubbs Café.

"Everything was right in the middle of town," Ted said. "And there were so many people."

It was crowded enough for a street musician to try and make a go of it. He parked his convertible in front of Hubbs Café and would sit in the backseat strumming a guitar and singing.

"Nobody paid any attention to him," Ted said. "But I remember someone saying once, 'Who does he think he is? Vaughn Monroe?' "

Downtown Clinton also had two drugstores, a jewelry store, a bank, two service stations/auto-repair shops, and Joe's Pool Hall. And it had its own emergency-medical system, long before anyone could call 911.

Before there were cell towers, there were switchboard operators, who served as intermediaries between the caller and the recipient. Their office was upstairs above Cory Chapman's drugstore, near the Clinton Infirmary.

So, if you were calling for a doctor, the operator might look out the window and see Dr. Clovis walking across the street toward the hospital and inform you, "He should be back in his office in just a few minutes."

At one point, the McKnights had two stores on Main Street. We had two barbershops, too. And Fanny Powell had a beauty parlor.

Paul Hooge ran one barbershop, which was just off Main Street. Whatever success he had could be attributed, in part, to a low overhead. The wood was unpainted and some of it was rotten.

Newt Wright and Hardy Talbot manned the two-chair shop. We called Wright by his last name, and Hardy by his first.

You didn't have to need a haircut. Dominoes were popular, and competitive enough to draw outbursts of joy or agony.

If you were there strictly for business, you knew that Wright was more advanced in that he could do a flattop, a cut that Hardy never mastered.

My strongest memory from the barber shop was a conversation, not a cut. While I was waiting for either Wright or Hardy to finish, another customer asked me who my favorite Clinton football player was. At the time, it was fullback Francis Hunt.

Harry Bunch, who was in Hardy's chair, took it from there. He started talking about what physical harm he planned to perpetrate against Francis – obviously, for my benefit. And it worked. I remember fearing for Francis' safety, until Wright told me that Harry liked to kid. What a relief.

When I told the story to Francis years later, he just laughed. "Harry was one of my best friends," he said. "He was always joking."

Harry was also an outstanding athlete in his own right. But you wouldn't have guessed it by looking, unless you were looking at him on the track, where he starred in the hurdles and high jump.

"I can remember in the 12th grade Harry was entered in five individual events," John Allen Phares said. "I can't remember anybody else doing that. They might have entered five events counting relays, but not five individual events."

Harry's best event was the high jump. And few jumpers have ever been so confident.

He often would pass on the lower jumps until much of the competition had been eliminated. Then, when there were just a couple of jumpers left, he would take off his warmups, ease up to the bar, and scissor-kick over it.

His success often was celebrated with a cigarette – out of the sight of coach Hubert Polk.

"When you thought about Harry, you thought about somebody smoking a cigarette or drinking a beer," John Allen said. "And he looked like a 75-year-old man. But he was a great athlete."

Based on that characterization, Harry probably spent some time in Joe's Pool Hall. Some people best remember Joe's place for the air conditioner, rather than the pool or bar. The unit had no cover, so you could see the air blowing across the room like a fog.

Henry Forrester was a regular at Joe's. His finest moment occurred in the line of fire.

When the town's fire siren sounded in the middle of the night, Joe's patrons scrambled outside with one exception, according to Ted's secondhand account.

The fire siren apparently was Mr. Henry's cue to deliver a brief Shakespearean soliloquy. He stretched out his arm and loudly proclaimed, "Let it burn!"

After finishing his theatrics, he joined the others outside. That's when he learned his own house was the one on fire.

Just off Main Street, there were the Clinton Infirmary and Joy Theatre on the east side of the courthouse. Both were usually busy - for obviously different reasons.

William F. Kline Jr. began his law practice in downtown Clinton in 1960. His father, William F. Kline Sr., who had died the year before when his son was finishing up law school, had a great reputation, which made it easier for Mr. Billy.

"Several people came up to me and said 'Your daddy was kind to me, so I'll take a chance on you,' " Mr. Billy said.

He had a challenging case right away. His new client wanted to get back the $100 he paid for a mule.

Why? Because the mule had blind teeth.

Obviously, Mr. Billy's first question was: "What are blind teeth?"

His client said the mule had an extra set of teeth in the back of his mouth, so he couldn't take a bit properly, which meant he couldn't be adequately controlled.

After a cram course in "blind teeth," Mr. Billy won the case. In fact, he won a lot of cases, and later became a longtime judge in East Feliciana Parish.

On the west side of the courthouse was another string of businesses. Top Jackson had a television repair shop. Sheriff Arch Doughty had an appliance store. Frank Haynes, who made his money in the sawmill business, had a Ford dealership for a while. Buddy Graham bought the hardware store when I was 9. The same year, my friend and classmate, Phil Graham, went to work in his daddy's newly acquired business.

A block off Main Street, on the north side of the courthouse, was historic Lawyer's Row, renowned for its architecture and longevity. The library was part of that. And the library was part of my family.

My grandmother, Sarah Dean, worked there as a volunteer. Later, we had the Audubon Regional Library.

There was another string of stores on the south side of the courthouse, which served all East Feliciana Parish. You didn't have to go to the library to get a book. The bookmobile brought books to rural areas throughout the parish.

Mother went to work there as a paid employee when I was a teenager. She manned the front desk, but her degree was in English. Since she didn't have a degree in library science, she couldn't be the head librarian. That always bothered me, but she seemed fine with her role.

She didn't retire until she was 74. She would have worked longer if there had been a part-time position. But it was fulltime or nothing. She suffered too much from chronic asthma to keep working five days a week.

After Mother retired, I probably went in the library only once or twice. When I think about the library now, I imagine myself opening the front door and seeing my mother look up from her desk. That memory is still uplifting, just as it was then - when I was in high school and Mother was healthy enough to work five days a week.

The library wasn't the only building downtown where I felt at home. I could go in the Graham's hardware store or McKnight's Department Store and feel the same way.

Many of those downtown buildings are still standing. But the people that made Clinton so special to me are missing.

I'm not the only one who misses them.

Not that long ago, when Louis McKnight and I were talking about the downtown Clinton of our youth, he said, "I wish we could go back for just one day and everything would be the same."

A Brick for Christmas

Not everybody went downtown to shop. After all, you didn't have to buy something to make the trip worthwhile.

I realized that at a young age. As an aspiring journalist, I could appreciate the breaking news as well as the human-interest stories that were available downtown.

The Graham's hardware store was well located if you were looking for human drama. The town jail was nearby.

Painters routinely frequented the hardware store. One of the regulars did his painting at East Louisiana State Hospital.

Fate Jarrell had more on his mind than paint on one trip to the hardware store, Phil Graham soon noticed.

"He kept cowering down and looking out the front of the store at his truck," Phil said.

Finally, he told Phil that one of the patients had gotten out of the hospital and asked for a ride. Fate obliged.

The passenger wanted a cigarette as much as he did a ride. Again, Fate met his request.

Then, the rider asked for another cigarette and another. But he never doused the ones he already had.

When Phil looked out the front window, he could see the man had four active cigarettes in his mouth.

Although there was no law against smoking multiple cigarettes, Phil added up the evidence – a man who had just left a mental institute had a mouth full of lit cigarettes – and concluded that a call to the jailhouse was justified.

Deputy Albert Moffit answered the call and told Phil to escort the strange smoker to jail. Phil reviewed the evidence again and decided that was a horrible idea.

"You have to come and get him," Phil said.

Moffit did just that. He brought three trustees with him, which made Phil feel even better about his decision not to follow Moffit's first suggestion.

Phil also picked up on jailhouse gossip, not all of which he could confirm. For example, there was the "quick-draw" story.

As town marshal John Manchester and Moffit were sitting in the jail, Manchester kept asking if Moffit wanted to see his quick draw. But when time came to exhibit his handgun prowess, the demonstration didn't go as planned. Manchester dropped his gun, which went off. The bullet supposedly glanced off the concrete floor and began ricocheting around the jailhouse.

Neither Manchester nor Moffit was injured.

Manchester was too tolerant for his job or his own good. Teenagers capitalized repeatedly on his shortcoming.

They once painted the flashing light atop his pickup green. Another time, while he was dining in the Snack Shack, they rallied their forces to lift Manchester's car and lower the rear axle down on top of coke cases.

Then, one of the pranksters peeled out in front of the Snack Shack while Manchester was still inside. As they figured, Manchester rushed back to his car. But when he shifted into reverse to begin pursuit, the wheels spun in place, and the car went nowhere.

Downtown pranks were usually more verbal. And folks didn't mind paying for them.

Billy Joe Yarbrough discovered that as a kid when he frequented Mr. Joe Felps' garage. He worked for about a quarter an insult.

For example, when Monroe Hatcher saw school superintendent Pat Dupruy on the sidewalk across the street, he would give Billy his assignment, which the young entrepreneur would swiftly carry out.

"I'd run over there to Mr. Dupruy and say, 'You old son of a bitch,' " Billy said.

Right away, Mr. Dupruy knew where the message originated. He looked over to the garage and shouted, "You're ruining this boy, Monroe."

But as Mr. Dupruy walked off, Billy could see that he was laughing.

Paid insults didn't start with Billy. In fact, they were popular a generation earlier.

When Mr. Ikey McKnight was a kid, he played Billy's role. Harry Carroll, who ran a general store on Main Street, would pay him to insult whomever he thought needed insulting.

No one was off limits, including Mr. Ikey.

"Daddy told me this story," Ted Chaney said. "He said Harry Carroll told Ikey he had a Christmas present for him."

Ikey didn't open his unexpected gift in the store. Instead, he went across the street to the Courthouse Square, sat down on the grass and removed the wrapping from a package whose weight must have piqued his curiosity.

When the paper had been peeled away, Ikey could see his present was a brick. And Mr. Harry was able to watch him open it from his store across the street.

The joke didn't kill Mr. Ikey's sense of humor, which became legendary to those who frequented McKnight's Department store – or to any children who sought Halloween candy in his neighborhood.

Trick-or-treat ventures were prevalent in almost every neighborhood during my childhood. Johnny McConnell remembered that they could be extra scary if you visited Mr. Ikey's house.

"He would hide in the bushes outside his house and jump out to scare trick-or-treaters when they came by," Johnny said.

A sense of humor was almost a necessity for anyone who spent much time at McKnight's – or anywhere else downtown for that matter. And you didn't have to wait for Halloween to experience a trick.

"That kind of stuff went on all day long," Ted said. "A lot of these men had businesses, but they had somebody else managing them."

So, they could afford to hang out at Mr. Joe's garage and work at entertaining themselves and their friends.

At the end of a work day, J. M. "Lit" Stewart's liquor store was a popular gathering place, located at the intersection of Plank Road and Main Street.

You could get gas out front or go inside for liquor. The gas and liquor had a price. The insults were free. Mr. Lit delivered them with the timing of a professional comedian and without changing his expression or raising his voice.

"It's a wonder he had any business," said his son, John Irwin, who witnessed many of the insults firsthand.

John Irwin remembers a new customer with long hair checking Mr. Lit's inventory.

"Hey, fellah, you're in the wrong place," Mr. Lit said. "The barbershop is down the street on the right."

Another time, a customer took his time checking the various bottles on the shelves. Too much time, Mr. Lit decided.

"If you want to read, go down to the library or the courthouse," Mr. Lit told him.

Local comedians didn't account for all the entertainment. There also was the Joy Theatre across the street from the Courthouse Square.

I have two strong memories of the Joy Theatre. One was bad. The other was tragic.

You think "Gone with the Wind" was a long movie? You should have seen it at the Joy Theatre. The projector failed repeatedly. It was "Long Gone with the Wind." With all the delays, the movie must have lasted over five hours.

Miss Hodges worked the ticket office. Her husband's main job was at the sawmill, but he would pick her up when the theater closed.

Mr. and Mrs. Hodges were sitting in their car parked in front of Felps' garage near the theater, which they had just closed for the evening, when he was shot to death. There were numerous rumors about what happened. Some thought a local person was involved. Others said the killer was a stranger passing through town.

Despite all the speculation about who did it and how he escaped, the murder was never solved. The theater was closed shortly after Mr. Hodges' death in 1959, and the Hodges family moved to Baton Rouge.

The Joy Theatre was reopened again in the 1960s, but it wasn't the same. By then, folks had gotten accustomed to going to Baton Rouge, where they could see new movies - long before they came to Clinton – at the Paramount, Gordon or Hart theaters. The Joy Theatre closed for good in the late 1960s.

An improved Plank Road had something to do with that. Once it was straightened and smoothed out, the drive to Baton Rouge was a breeze compared to the old days when the bumps were substantial enough to knock out your fillings.

An improved Plank Road didn't take away business from McKnight's Department Store. In fact, there was enough business for two stores in the late 1950s.

Mr. Clay and Miss Jeannette McKnight opened the original store on a corner on the south side of Main Street. Their sons, Louis (Skeet) and Ikey, both worked in the store until they opened a second McKnight's on the same side of the street. Both stores featured a wide assortment of men's and women's clothing and shoes.

Mr. Louis' wife, Peggy; and Mr. Ikey's wife, Marquita, also worked in the store. As their children grew older, they joined the work force, too.

"We all got along," said Shirley, Mr. Louis' and Miss Peggy's daughter. "Even when I went to work at Silliman (school), I would still work at the store on Saturdays."

Christmas Eve was one of their biggest days. Since some people preferred to do their shopping at the last minute, McKnight's was always open the day before Christmas.

"We would stay open as long as there were shoppers," Shirley said.

McKnight's Department Store was the main gathering place in downtown Clinton.

McKnight's always was as much about socializing as shopping. Almost everyone in the store was a good conversationalist. There were chairs and a coffee pot in the back.

You could talk art with Miss Marquita or politics with Mr. Ikey, who never let business get in the way of a political debate. My mother loved discussing national and local politics with him.

The conversation changed during the day depending on who was doing the talking. My mother; my cousin, Sue Record; and Evelyn Kline were late afternoon regulars. But I can remember listening to a wide range of characters like Frank Haynes, Bill Ourso, Morgan Montgomery, Buck Powell and Moffit. Many of the male conversations centered around sports, especially LSU football.

Mr. Ikey had a great recall for LSU plays, good and bad. So did his son, "Little Ikey."

They even used their LSU connection to enhance business. One Saturday after football season, McKnight's had LSU stars Billy Cannon and Johnny Robinson signing autographs.

Despite Clinton's proximity to Tiger Stadium, not everyone was an LSU fan. We were only about 20 miles from Mississippi. In the late 1950s, when Ole Miss was a national power, Clinton also had its share of Rebels fans, all of whom Mr. Ikey loved needling, which he could do even in defeat.

Mr. Morgan was one of his favorite targets. Mr. Ikey loved telling the story of how Mr. Morgan changed his football allegiance.

One fall Saturday, Mr. Morgan drove to Tiger Stadium with the intent of buying a ticket outside the stadium. However, he was so incensed over the high prices scalpers demanded for tickets, he returned to Clinton an Ole Miss fan.

At least, that was Mr. Ikey's explanation.

The McKnights treated their regular customers like family. You could see that in the photos that were displayed in a glass case in the back of the store.

Those photos meant more the older I got and the further away from Clinton my career took me. And I can't remember returning to Clinton without stopping by McKnight's.

It was similar to going back in time, and I mean that in the best way. As long as the McKnight family was in that store, a part of the hometown I cherished was still intact.

Sometimes, as I left the store and drove away, memories returned. Then, I could see Mr. Ikey, hands on hips, telling the story of how Mr. Morgan became an Ole Miss fan.

His smile broadened as he went along. By the time he finished, his smile had turned to laughter.

That's how I like to remember downtown Clinton.

One More Spin

A common lament of any young person living in a small town: "There's nothing to do here."

I guess that depends on what you want to do. You couldn't tour a museum in Clinton. Or go to an art gallery. Or attend a professional sporting event.

But even back in the 1950s and 60s, we had an entertainment complex, just outside the city limits on the Liberty Highway. We just didn't call it an "entertainment complex."

The fair came every year. There was a race track, which could accommodate sprinters, quarter horses or even cars. Pretty Creek, a popular swimming hole, was nearby. There also was a grandstand; a baseball field, which is now named after Man Williams; and the American Legion Hall, a multi-purpose facility, which seemingly will outlast us all.

When we held our 50-year class reunion at the Legion Hall, a large disco ball was still on display, reminding us that we had changed far more than the Legion Hall had.

If you wanted to dance, the Legion Hall was the place to go. And if you didn't want to dance but had no choice, the Legion Hall also was the place to go.

As a kid, I didn't see the importance of learning how to do the Foxtrot, Mambo, or Cha-cha. But mother enrolled me in a dance class at the Legion Hall one September. Although I can't remember ever putting my dance education to much use, I still remember some steps, like: "one, two – cha-cha-cha."

Someone might have been bold enough to do "the alligator" on a Saturday night at the Legion Hall, but I never saw anyone try the Cha-cha. And there was more apt to be a fight than a Foxtrot.

Chaperones had a set protocol for managing physical confrontations: "Take it outside." While that didn't discourage fighting, it made sure there was no collateral damage to the Legion Hall.

Watching Dick Freeman dance was as entertaining as a fight to some.

"He had such an unusual dance style, Joan Yarbrough was the only one who could dance with him," Ronnie Feierabend said. "When he would slow dance, he could dip really low, then turn a circle on his tiptoes and lean way back.

"I had never seen anyone dance like that. It was a production."

Confidence probably had something to do with Dick's success as a dancer. He wasn't shy about his singing ability, either.

"Even as a kid, he was always saying that he could sing better than Elvis Presley," Billy Andrews said.

Dick never reached the heights of The King, but he lasted longer. In his 70s, he was still singing in Branson, Mo.

The Legion Hall occasionally drew name bands from Baton Rouge. Van Broussard made an appearance. So did John Fred and The Playboys, who had a hit with "Judy in Disguise."

Not all the dances were for teenagers. The Clintonians formed an adult dance club. Since liquor was sold at their dances, you had to be 18 to attend.

That didn't keep Ronnie from listening.

"They always had a good band," he said. "Before I was old enough to go, we went and sat out on cars and listened to the bands play.

"All the 'beautiful people' in Clinton went. I always thought Gloria Powell was the most beautiful woman in Clinton. I had a crush on her."

The Clintonians usually held their dances in the winter since the Legion Hall wasn't air-conditioned. Some of our other entertainment was seasonal, too.

The fair came in the fall. A skating rink was available in the summer.

Linda Kay Fultz said she and Christine Overton both broke an arm when they fell at the skating rink. On the same day. What are the odds?

"I don't know what Christine's problem was, but I couldn't skate," Linda Kay said.

Her parents brought that up when she told them she wanted to go skating

"You don't know anything about skating," they told her. "You will go down there and break your arm."

She did just that. And the last people she wanted to tell were her parents.

"I didn't tell them for about a week," she said. "I just tried to use my other arm as much as possible."

Finally, when the swelling became too noticeable and the pain too annoying, Linda Kay gave in.

Sophomore quarterback Amile deGeneres injured his ankle at the same rink. His coach, Hubert Polk, was furious – at the skating rink, not Amile.

The skating rink didn't have the history that the fair did. Artie Barnett remembers attending the fair in the 1930s.

"Ladies would enter embroidery, jellies, and preserves in contests," Miss Artie said. "The winners would get a blue ribbon.

"We would get the day off from school to go to the fair. The first time I ever ate barbecue was at the fair."

A 1930s fair probably wasn't that much different from the 1950s fairs that I attended.

I made my fair debut at about 10. Right away, I realized what a big deal it was.

School was let out for a day so students could attend. Buses that usually took kids to school took them to the fair instead.

"Fair Day" was one of the longest of the year, because once you ran out of money what could you do while waiting for your ride home? Some had more to lose than others.

Hadley Hudnall earned money by picking up pecans for his neighbor in the fall. The timing was perfect.

"The fair would come a week after the pecans," he said. "So, I would have 10 or 12 dollars."

Year after year, the results never changed. Whatever he made picking up pecans, he spent at the fair.

My fair debut went OK until I discovered a spinning wheel, managed by a woman that I remember having gypsy-like looks. She obviously was part of the attraction. And a 10-year-old was terribly overmatched against her salesmanship.

I was convinced I really had a shot at winning a multi-colored switchblade knife. So, I kept handing her quarters. She kept handing me worthless trinkets in return.

Even as I stashed one trinket after another in a pants pocket, I felt exhilarated at the next spin of the wheel, which eventually came to rest at another trinket.

Having spent my last quarter, I remained hopeful, as any gambling addict might. I proceeded to walk the grounds, looking down the entire time. I was rewarded for my determination. After finding two quarters, I returned to the gypsy woman. She seemed as happy as I was.

Why wouldn't she? We were in it together.

I spun the wheel two more times. And won two more trinkets.

I weighed the odds of finding another quarter before going to Plan B. I found my mother, who was nearby, and begged for more money. She declined, but I kept begging. I even led her to the gypsy woman's spinning wheel.

I remember experiencing a sinking sensation when I realized my mother wasn't as impressed with my new friend. Nor was she dazzled by the multi-colored switchblade knife.

She took my hand and led me away. I was on the verge of tears.

I lost more than quarters at the fair.

A couple of years later, I had my shell collection on exhibit at the fair. Why? I have no idea. And it wasn't as though I scoured desolate beaches for the shells. I bought them at a Mississippi Gulf Coast gift shop.

Nonetheless, I was proud of the exhibit. So was the person who stole my shell collection.

The worst part was that it included my prize shell, which was white with leopard spots.

What else do I remember about the fair? There was an airborne ride, whose individual compartments were just big enough for one person. You were swung around like a spinning wheel and tilted back and forth often enough until you became nauseated. The ride seemingly lasted for several minutes, or until one of the paying passengers screamed that he was about to throw up.

On one occasion, I was the screamer.

With a couple of exceptions, my experiences at the adjacent baseball field were more pleasant.

An experienced Little League infielder, though not a particularly good one, I found myself in left field for one practice. I felt uncomfortable on the foreign ground as Mr. Moffit knocked a fly-ball my way.

Despite the discomfort in my new surroundings, I judged the ball almost perfectly. I settled in to make the catch and held my glove in front of my face.

The ball sailed an inch over my glove, striking me above the left eye, which was swollen shut almost immediately. So ended my career as a left fielder. And so ended my practice.

Mr. Moffit took me home, and Mother met us at the door. Since there was nothing wrong with my right eye, I could see she was horrified at the sight of a purple budge where my left eye was supposed to be.

Half smiling, Mr. Moffit assured Mother I would be fine. Her look said, "Oh, you're a doctor now?"

I couldn't see out of the eye for two days.

My other baseball mishap at the Legion Field park wasn't nearly as severe and came after my career had advanced to the Babe Ruth League stage.

Mother had been nice enough to buy me a new glove the previous weekend. It bore Rocky Colavito's signature but was distinguished by the six fingers and bigger trap. I didn't even know there was such a thing as a six-finger glove. Very cool.

Two problems, though: (1) An illness had deprived us of our first baseman; (2) Stuart Chaney was at shortstop.

Stuart, who was two years older, had the strongest arm I ever encountered on a baseball field. And, as the stand-in first baseman, I had to receive his throws.

It took only one throw for me to realize my new glove had a significant drawback. It had virtually no padding. Catching the ball in the pocket of the glove was akin to catching it with my barehand. I tried to catch everything in the trap, which resulted in a few misses. I could live with that.

I really enjoyed baseball – in part, because of our coach, James "Red" McDowell. He had a passion for the game that was contagious. He also was a creative thinker. And a great communicator.

After Louis McKnight had reached first base to open an inning, Mr. Red gave him the steal sign from the dugout. Louis showed no recognition whatsoever.

Mr. Red gave the signal a second time. Again, Louis failed to respond.

A new strategy was required, Mr. Red reasoned. He wrote, "steal second" on a piece of paper and had a player deliver the message to Louis at first base.

"I stole second on the next pitch," Louis said. "I think I still have that note in a scrapbook."

Mr. Red didn't miss much - in a game or practice.

Once, when we were taking infield practice before a game with St. Francisville, the opposing players were heckling us terribly. Mr. Red called the infielders together and gave specific instructions to the first and second baseman.

After fielding the next ground ball, the second baseman threw the ball as hard as he could to first. As instructed, the first baseman made no attempt to catch it. St. Francisville players scrambled to get out of the way as the ball sailed into the dugout.

They quieted down after that.

One Little League season, Mr. Red introduced us to revolutionary uniforms: red baseball caps, white shirts and red shorts. Yes, shorts.

We greeted the uniforms with curiosity. Our opponents greeted them with derisive laughter.

Maybe, that was Mr. Red's intention. In my career as a sports columnist, I've encountered numerous coaches who love to create an us-against-the-world mentality for their team. As trite as that might seem, players usually respond to it.

Maybe, we did, too, because we won more than we lost.

Mr. Red also made sure we got specialized instruction. For example, he had umpire Ben Price at one of our practices.

"We were practicing tagging people out at second," second baseman Warren Record remembered. "I missed a tag, and Mr. Ben dressed me down."

"You've got to act like you got him," Mr. Ben stressed. "You can't give away that you didn't make the tag."

The following week, Clinton was playing St. Francisville, and Mr. Ben was the umpire. Warren was prepared to put his newfound baseball education to work.

"I missed the tag by a mile at second," Warren said.

But he didn't act like he had missed the tag. Mr. Ben signaled the last out of the game, which Clinton won.

"Some of the fans came out after the game," Warren said. "I thought they were going to assassinate Mr. Ben."

On the way off the field, Mr. Ben approached Warren and asked him if he made the tag.

"No sir, I missed him a mile," Warren said.

"I've got to live with these people," Mr. Ben said.

"But, Mr. Ben, you told me to do that."

"But not to me," he said.

Baseball at the Legion Field was a summer thing. But the fairgrounds also served us well during the school year. That's where we had our Parish Rally, pitting track athletes of all ages from Clinton against Jackson.

It was a big deal. School was let out for the day, and track athletes from LSU came up from Baton Rouge to work the events.

Clinton High's track athletes also practiced at the fairgrounds, which featured a half-mile track with limited visibility on the far side.

Horse races were popular during the 1950s. There were stables, grandstands, and even iron starting blocks for the horses. The featured race usually had Frank Haynes' horse against Conrad Hooge's horse.

John Allen had a great location for all the action at our entertainment complex.

"When I was a kid, we had a little old white-frame house right there where the blacktop ran into the gravel," he said. "That was the entrance to the fairgrounds."

John Allen capitalized on the location.

"One day after the horse races, I was just messing around," John Allen said. "They had a rail that went around the track. On one of the posts, there was a little nail. Hanging on the nail was a 20-dollar bill."

He found $20 hanging on a nail at the fairgrounds. And I spent my year's savings without getting so much as a switchblade knife at the same venue.

So unfair.

Aren't You Paul Newman?

"The Dukes of Hazzard" was filmed in Clinton in 2005 but you won't hear much about it from older Clintonians. They're jaded when it comes to movies.

While the movie did OK at the box office, critics weren't kind to a film that featured Jessica Simpson in her screen-acting debut, country music legend Willie Nelson and past-his-prime Burt Reynolds.

Of that casting, critic Robert Ebert wrote, "Of course, you don't have to be smart to get into the 'Dukes of Hazzard.' But people like Willie Nelson and Burt Reynolds should have been smart enough to stay out of it.

"Here is a lame-brained, outdated wheeze about a couple of good ol' boys who roar around the back roads of the South in the General Lee, their beloved 1969 Dodge Charger.

"As it happens, I also drove a 1969 Dodge Charger. You could have told them apart because mine did not have a Confederate flag painted on the roof."

I could go on quoting the famed critic, but there are no plot twists in his assessment of a movie based on a successful TV series that I'm proud to say I never saw.

As scathing as Ebert's critique was, at least he was kind enough to see the movie before he bashed it. My friends in Clinton expected the worst while the movie was being filmed. Nor were they enamored with Simpson, who, according to reports from McKnight's Department Store, had the appeal of a spoiled brat. A popular characterization was a "stuck-up bitch." Willie Nelson said, "She didn't get spanked enough as a child," in trying to explain her behavior to the locals.

My friend, Randy Peay was one of the movie's harshest critics, as I would have expected. Later, when the TV series, "Duck Dynasty," was at its peak in popularity, I asked Randy if he watched it. He smirked and said, "If I want to watch someone blow up a beaver dam, I'll follow Bubby Jackson around."

Randy was biased about "Dukes of Hazzard," because the driver of a movie truck had made the mistake of blocking Randy's car.

"I'll move it in just a minute," the driver told Randy, who was then operating his accounting firm in the back of his family's furniture store on Main Street.

Randy could have waited quietly, but that wasn't his style. Instead, he used those few minutes to tell the driver that no one in Clinton was impressed that Hollywood was bringing "The Dukes of the Hazzard" to town.

"Let me tell you something," said Randy, who so often began his commentary with those five words. "We had Joanne Woodward, Paul Newman, and Orson Welles here for 'The Long, Hot Summer.' Nobody here cares about Jessica Simpson or 'The Dukes of Hazzard.' "

My guess is he pointed a forefinger at the truck driver for added emphasis.

"The Long, Hot Summer" is where Clinton's movie snobbery began. Numerous other movies would be filmed in Clinton – most of them far better than "The Dukes of Hazzard."

"The Free State of Jones," starring Matthew McConaughey, was filmed in Clinton in 2016. About the same time, 10 miles away, another movie company had turned an East Feliciana Parish pasture into a Mexican town for the filming of a "Magnificent Seven" remake, starring Denzel Washington.

But neither movie could compete with "The Long, Hot Summer" in the minds of those old enough to remember when it brought some of Hollywood's biggest stars to Clinton in 1957. The cast included Woodward, Newman, Welles, Angela Lansbury, Lee Remick, and Tony Franciosa.

Woodward, Newman, and Welles all won Academy Awards. Lansbury was nominated three times for best supporting actress, and Remick was nominated for best actress for her performance in "Days of Wine and Roses" in 1962.

Woodward was the biggest star at the time, though. She had just won the Academy Award for best actress for her portrayal of three different personalities – Eve White, Eve Black, and Jane – in "The Three Faces of Eve." Her role in "The Long, Hot Summer" wasn't as complicated. And, as Clara Varner – the daughter of wealthy southern parents – the dialect came easy for a woman who grew up in Thomasville, Ga., and graduated in drama from Louisiana State University.

The southern accent wasn't natural for Newman, who arrived ahead of the crew to study the speech of the natives. So, he didn't keep to himself.

One of his first stops was The Watchman, Clinton's weekly paper, and the paper of record for East Feliciana. After he met the owners, Roland and Malva Huson, he followed Roland to Joe's Pool Hall on Main Street. Newman had a few beers and met more locals, then ended up spending the night on the Huson's couch.

While Newman was busy socializing, he wanted to keep the movie a secret as long as he could. He first introduced himself as Ben Snopes. The alias didn't last long with the Husons, but they emphasized to their two children, Roland Jr. and Gadget, to keep "Paul Newman is in town" a secret.

The secret didn't survive a Friday night football game at Clinton High School.

Orson Welles (behind the wheel) and Paul Newman in Clinton's most famous movie, "The Long, Hot Summer."

Elaine Roddy looked through the stands and told a friend, "Look at that man. He looks just like Paul Newman." Molly Prestridge took it a step further. "Aren't you Paul Newman?" she asked the stranger. "No, I'm Ben Snopes," he said.

Mary Lillian Pullig also remembers seeing Newman at the game. "I looked into his brilliantly blue eyes and realized this man was not from Clinton," she said.

By then, his cover was blown. And Clinton had figured out a movie was coming to town.

But the movie star still had no trouble fitting in. He played pitch-and-catch with kids on the Courthouse Square, judged a local beauty pageant, and had a beer or two or three with the locals. It wasn't unusual to see him with a church key (for opening beer cans) hanging around his neck.

Newman probably became less interested in the locals when the rest of the cast arrived. Never mind that he was married with three children. Newman and Woodward suddenly had become Hollywood's hottest couple.

In January of 1958, soon after the movie was completed, Newman's wife, Jackie Witte, finally granted him a divorce, and he and Woodward were married. Their romantic partnership remained one of Hollywood's most famous marriages until Newman died in 2008.

The folks in Clinton didn't have to double date with Newman and Woodward to figure out there was an attraction between the two that didn't end when Ben Quick (Newman's character) and Clara left the set. Even 13-year-olds noticed.

"We would hide in the bushes and watch them between sets," Johnny McConnell said. "They would be making out on the picnic blanket they spread out on the church grounds."

Although the local populace got to know Newman better than the rest of the cast, most of the actors enjoyed fitting in. They played softball games at the Fairgrounds, attended a steak dinner at the home of Sheriff Arch Doughty and his wife, Elaine. And Newman and Woodward had dinner regularly at Nell Haynes' house.

"I had an option of staying at home for the dinner or going to the fair," said Kathy Doughty, who was 10 when her parents hosted the cast. "I chose the fair.

"When I got home, Lee Remick was sitting in the middle of the living room floor playing dolls with my sister, Denise."

Kathy said her father's lasting memory of the dinner was Newman's appetite. "I thought he was going to OD on corn on the cob," he told her.

The sheriff contributed more than a steak dinner to the movie. He also supplied a jeep, which served as "Big Daddy's" primary mode of transportation. But it looked different in the movie than when the movie was being made.

"Orson Welles (who played Big Daddy) didn't drive the jeep," Kathy said. "They were pulling it with another vehicle. They had to tow it everywhere."

Memories of the movie have been reinforced many times since on television. You might not get "Dukes of Hazzard" on "Turner's Classic Movies," but "The Long, Hot Summer" was close enough to classic to get air time.

Carmen Peay remembered not being able to sleep one night, so she turned on the television and flipped through the channels. A familiar movie got her attention. "The Long, Hot Summer" had just started.

Once again, she could see her mother along with other locals running through downtown Clinton as a barn burned in the background.

In fact, the barn was nowhere near Clinton's Main Street. That was just movie magic. The barn belonged to Mahoney Perkins. And the Perkins were among the biggest winners of the movie. They got paid for a barn that was barely standing.

"It was basically falling down," Tommy Perkins, the oldest of the Perkins' two sons, said. "We were going to have to tear it down."

As it turned out, Hollywood paid them to tear it down, which qualifies as one of the best movie deals in Clinton history.

There was far more to the project than tearing down and building up a barn. The movie crew was there for a week, waiting on just the right background.

"They set up trailers for the stars, and they had 18-wheelers with movie gear, cameras, and lights," Tommy said. "They were waiting on blue skies and white clouds, because that's what they wanted to use for the background when the opening credits were shown."

Newman and Woodward took advantage of the free time. They rode Mr. Perkins' cattle horses while the other stars were sitting in lawn chairs waiting for the perfect sky to show up.

Woodward liked the horse she was riding so much that Newman offered to buy it from the Perkins. But when Newman's proposal came up for discussion at dinner, Tommy's younger brother, Billy, nixed the deal.

"That was Billy's horse, Pal," Tommy said. "I don't remember how much money they offered, but Billy wouldn't sell him."

Once the barn was presentable and the background was suitable for the silver screen, the burning didn't take long. About 15 minutes, Tommy said.

The St. Andrews Episcopal Church grounds served as the most popular movie setting if you were looking for friends and family members with bit parts. They gathered there for the filming of a church bazaar. Children got social security cards and were paid about $20 a day for just being movie extras. Others had bigger parts.

Donnie Phares still remembers the instructions he and his young friends were given for the bazaar scene. "Go run around," they were told. Wonder if that's how Meryl Streep got her start?

While Tommy Perkins was just a spectator when the barn went up in flames, he played a more strategic role at the church.

"I was a human mark," Tommy said. "They set me out there and (told the actors) to pivot and turn at the kid with the big ears."

Mary Munson was selected as a stand-in for Woodward since they had similar complexions. But they didn't share the same status. Munson would sit in the sun while the crew set up camera angles and settings. Woodward stayed in the shade, presumably with Newman nearby.

The movie's title was misleading if you were there for the filming. It was filmed in the fall, from Sept. 23 through Oct. 21. And in late October, it sometimes was cool enough that some of the local participants brought sweaters, which they donned between scenes.

The temperature wasn't the biggest problem. It rained 13 days while the movie was being filmed.

After the movie was produced, Woodward got top billing – not surprising since she had just won an Academy Award.

"The Long, Hot Summer" was followed by another Clinton movie two years later. Raymond Burr and Martha Hyer starred in "Desire in the Dust." The theme was familiar.

You had another southern town, a dysfunctional family and a drifter up to no good.

In "The Long, Hot Summer," Newman played a barn-burning menace. In "Desire," Ken Scott played an ex-con whose criminal background didn't include barn burning. He ended up getting chased by hounds.

Burr's character was the equivalent of Welles' but not nearly as well received by the critics. As a New York Times review put it, "Mr. Burr is a pale, mumbling counterpart of Orson Welles in "Summer."

Burr came off better in the reviews from Joe's Pool Hall. He supposedly could match Newman when it came to beer drinking, consuming an entire case in an evening. Nobody remembers much about Welles, except that he either couldn't or wouldn't drive a car.

Newman returned to Clinton in 1989 to film a few scenes in the movie, "Blaze," in which he portrayed former Louisiana Gov. Earl K. Long. I could relate to his performance because I remember listening to Long deliver a campaign speech on the Courthouse Square. My conclusion: Newman's Long wasn't as crazy as the real one, but he had prettier eyes.

The scenes were filmed at the old Clinton High School. In one scene, it was the Mandeville State Mental Institute. In another, it was a French Quarter restaurant.

Newman wasn't as sociable in his brief return to Clinton. Maybe, he just didn't have the time. But Nell Haynes didn't wait for him to come visit her. She supposedly barged in on a scene at the high school, and shouted Newman's name. Sure enough, he remembered her.

In 1966, the movie, "Alvarez Kelly," brought other famous actors to Clinton. The Civil War drama starred Richard Widmark and William Holden, who was returning to the screen after a two-year absence. Based on movie critics, the former Academy Award winner's return didn't go well.

"Sounder," starring Cicely Tyson and Paul Winfield was filmed in Clinton in 1972. It was a box-office hit and received an Academy Award nomination for Best Picture. Also, Winfield was nominated for Best Actor.

In 1972, the made-for-TV movie, "Moon of the Wolf" was filmed in Clinton. The movie starred David Janssen, Barbara Rush, and Bradford Dillman – one of whom played a werewolf. Don't worry. I won't give it away.

But while movies have come and gone with varying degrees of success, none of them had the star power or staying power of "The Long, Hot Summer."

Phil Graham still has tangible evidence of the movie in his home. It's a table from the home of Miss Nell, his great aunt. He likes to think that Newman dined off that very table when Newman and Woodward had dinner at Miss Nell's.

"I call it my, 'Paul Newman table,' " he said.

But Clinton doesn't need furniture to remember the movie.

Billy Yarbrough can recall his vision of Lee Remick – her red hair and green eyes – as she stepped from a white limousine for a scene at the Courthouse Square. Roland Huson Jr. remembers how nervous he was trying to light a cigarette for Remick ("It's a wonder I didn't burn her nose off," he said). And Johnny McConnell still can tell you the name of Woodward's Chihuahua, El Chico, who was a fixture on the set.

Johnny, who always has been an animal lover, also remembered reading of El Chico's demise. He was run over when he jumped from Woodward's convertible into Southern California traffic.

But the Woodward-Newman union, like my hometown's memory of the "Long, Hot Summer," endured. A romance that heated up on a picnic blanket in Clinton, La., lasted 50 years.

Miss Opal's Clinic

My first impression of the Clinton Infirmary was formed under dire circumstances when I was only 6 years old.

I was sitting on my mother's bed with a thermometer in my mouth when I inexplicably clinched my teeth. The possibility of fever soon became a secondary problem.

Even in the early 1950s, it already had been determined that mercury shouldn't be ingested. Mother rushed me to the hospital, where someone with medical expertise pumped out my stomach. It was reassuring to know that, even in a town as small as Clinton, you could get your stomach pumped out whenever you chewed up a thermometer.

Not only could you get emergency medical care, you could get emergency surgery at the Clinton Infirmary. John Allen Phares remembers that the infirmary once served his friend, Don Brady, as both an emergency room and a surgical center.

Don had shot himself in the foot when a quick-draw contest took a wrong turn, according to John Allen. He said the .22 caliber gun went off before it cleared Don's holster.

John Allen got a firsthand report the next morning from Don, who had been admitted to the Clinton Infirmary.

"He said, 'I shot myself in the foot, and I'm scared to go home, ' " John Allen said.

John Allen arrived at the infirmary to see Don with his foot in a cast and elevated. But Don was more concerned about how his parents would react than the damage he had self-inflicted with his quick draw.

Don was even scared to call his parents, the toughest of whom was his mother. He asked John Allen to call on his behalf.

John Allen wanted no part of that. So, Don finally made the call. When Don's mother answered, he disguised his voice and asked, "Is Mr. Brady there?"

Later, John Allen realized that the infirmary could provide more than medical care.

When Clyde Lewis Carter graduated, John Allen was next in line for one of the most coveted jobs a Clinton teenager could have. He became a deliveryman for A-1 Cleaners, which was owned by Jake and Cloteil Breitung.

The job paid $7 a week with a $5 Christmas bonus. For that, you delivered clothes after school five days a week.

One day, when John Allen arrived for work, he was surprised that Miss Cloteil wasn't behind the counter. Told that she had gone to the infirmary, John Allen was so concerned that when he finished his deliveries, he went to check on her.

He was walking down the long corridor of the hospital when he saw Miss Cloteil coming toward him from the opposite end. She was wearing a nightgown and robe.

"What's wrong, Miss Cloteil?" John Allen asked.

"Oh, there's nothing wrong," she said.

"Then, what are you doing in the infirmary?"

"When I have a week off each year, I spend it in the infirmary. Don't you think if I live with Jake Breitung for 52 weeks a year, I deserve a week to myself?"

So, she checked into the infirmary for a one-week getaway.

My grandmother, who lived to be 95, spent the last year of her life in the infirmary. Since her health had worsened and mother could no longer care for her, the only other option would have been a nursing home. But Dr. Clovis told mother that my grandmother could have the other bed in the room with his ageing mother.

Before grandmother had to be hospitalized, Dr. Clovis visited us often to see how she was doing. He also offered academic advice when he saw me studying.

"Just memorize everything they throw at you," he said. "That's how I got through medical school."

Although it sounded good at the time, it didn't work with geometry.

At one time or another, I also was treated at the Clinton Infirmary by doctors Paul Jackson and Jack Pullig.

Dr. Pullig didn't take a direct route to medical practice. He was an acclaimed professor at Louisiana Tech, where he taught premed and laboratory science courses to future doctors. He was so good at his job that students told him he should go to medical school himself.

He was 34 years old when he decided to do just that. He moved to New Orleans with his wife, Rachel, and his two young children, Mary Lillian and Ginger.

Miss Rachel taught school in Algiers while her husband studied to become a doctor. Meanwhile, in the summer, he interned at the Clinton Infirmary, where he later began his practice.

As the new doctor on the staff, Dr. Pullig did the most traveling. After lunch, he would drive 20 miles to Greensburg, where he would see patients in the back of a drugstore.

He also made house calls along the way sometimes. Those house calls often took him far from paved roads, where waiting patients might tie a flag or put a tin pie pan on their mail box to help the doctor locate them.

"Janie Randolph was one of his patients," said Ginger, who sometimes accompanied him on distant house calls. "She was arthritic, and her family put everything she needed within reach.

"It was very difficult to get to her house. It was on a red-clay, dirt road way off Highway 10."

One winter day, Dr. Pullig decided to make an unplanned visit to his out-of-the-way patient. Neither she nor her relatives had called. Later, when telling the story, Dr. Pullig would say he "had a hunch."

As he neared the house, he saw smoke. When he went inside, his patient was still in bed. A log had rolled out of the fireplace, and the wood floor was about to become inflamed.

"The little pine cabin was probably just like kindling," Ginger said. "He saved her life."

The doctors weren't the only medical caregivers of note in Clinton. Anyone who ever visited the Clinton Infirmary probably remembers nurse Opal Chambers. I remember her as being bright, efficient, and inspiring confidence with anyone she was treating.

"People told me that she saved their lives," said Alice, Miss Opal's daughter. "They said she was the backbone of the hospital."

You also got the impression that Opal could have run the business side of the hospital, too.

A career in nursing wasn't Miss Opal's original plan, although she did go to nursing school. She and her longtime friend, Pauline Lawson, planned on becoming stewardesses.

"They went to nursing school together," Alice said. "Pauline talked her into working at the hospital to get a nest egg. Then, they would become stewardesses. You had to be an RN to be a stewardess then.

"But Pauline met George (Bunch) and Opal met McWillie (Chambers Jr.)."

And the Clinton Infirmary was the big winner.

Miss Opal grew up on a farm in Isabel, La., between Bogalusa and Franklinton. Her family didn't have the money to send her to college, but she was industrious. She worked in a shirt factory before she went to nursing school.

"She was really capable and smart," Alice said. "She wasn't very big, but – as they say in the country – she covered the ground she stood on."

She definitely had a presence. She also had a shrill voice that was unmistakable to anyone at the hospital.

A small hospital played to Miss Opal's strengths. Nurses performed tasks that interns and residents did in larger hospitals. And she welcomed the opportunity to develop different skills.

Dr. Jack Pullig taught her how to do X-rays, and she also did lab work. She and Miss Pauline, who was an anesthesiology nurse, teamed up in surgery.

Alice Chambers (left) and her mother, super-nurse Opal.

Since Miss Opal served as a surgical nurse, she sometimes had to rush to the hospital. Fortunately, it was a short, fast drive from her home on Bank Street to the hospital.

When my friend, Phil Graham, had emergency surgery to remove his spleen, Miss Opal was right there in the operating room, as Alice found out the next morning.

Alice didn't know anything about the surgery until her mother greeted her at breakfast, loudly proclaiming: "Well, Phil doesn't have a spleen anymore."

Her proximity to the hospital also benefited patients in an emergency. When Joe Felps' garage caught on fire, the hospital had to be evacuated since it was only a couple of buildings away. Miss Opal voluntarily sent patients to her home, which had six beds and a fold-out couch.

But she didn't bother telling McWillie what was coming his way.

Later, Alice asked him what he did when he saw the cars pulling up in the driveway, and the patients started coming in the house.

"I got out the big coffee pot," he said matter-of-factly.

Among Miss Opal's myriad of roles was matchmaker.

She once asked Mr. Easley, a patient in the hospital, what he needed. "A wife," said the man who was a widower.

He wasn't picky, he told Miss Opal.

"I can put up with just about anything," he said. "If she can make a good lemon meringue pie."

Ironically, a piemaker was in the next hospital room, Miss Opal quickly discovered. She told the lady the conversation she had just had with another patient.

"Well, I can make a good meringue pie, if I do say so myself," she said.

She then put on her slippers and visited the patient next door. They ended up getting married.

Miss Opal didn't always need a doctor beside her to diagnose a problem. Ruth Dart was grateful for that.

After being stung by wasps, Ruth had taken Benadryl and gone to sleep. When she woke up, her nose was closed off. She rushed to the hospital.

"Miss Opal saw me when I came in the door and pointed to the emergency room," Ruth said.

A resident doctor from Charity Hospital in New Orleans entered the room, just as Miss Opal was returning, needle in hand.

"Nurse, what are you doing?" he asked.

"I'm going to give this girl a shot or you're going to be performing a tracheotomy," she said.

Alice remembers her mother's instant diagnosis while watching the MacNeil/Lehr report on PBS.

"That man's going to have a heart attack," Miss Opal told Alice. "He's retaining fluid."

The next week, Jim Lehr had a heart attack.

Miss Opal often accompanied Dr. Clovis on house calls. She learned to appreciate his sense of humor along the way.

And she learned to appreciate how well he knew the community he served.

Miss Julia Dilly, who lived across the street from the high school when we were young, had a downhill drive leading onto Plank Road. Her idea of defensive driving was to blow the horn loudly as she roared down the driveway onto the highway.

"Watch this," Dr. Clovis told Miss Opal when he heard the horn as he approached Miss Dilly's driveway.

He knew what was about to happen. He kept going until he was only a few feet from her car, then slammed on the brake.

"Clovis Toler, didn't you hear me blowing the horn?" Miss Dilly exclaimed.

The Toler/Chambers medical partnership ended with Dr. Clovis' death. Miss Opal lost her job when the hospital changed hands.

"The new administration fired the experienced nurses and hired people for less money," Alice said. "Mother, Minnie Warm and Alice Curtis had more than 100 years in experience."

That might have worked out for the best in Miss Opal's case.

"They would have had to carry her out of there feet first," Alice said. "It was good for Momma to leave. She took art courses at LSU and traveled."

But she never stopped being a nurse.

Miss Opal was in a nursing home when she noticed another patient was struggling. Suddenly, it was as though she were back in the Clinton Infirmary ready to provide emergency medical care.

"Go get the nurse, this lady is having a stroke," she told one of the workers.

When the woman questioned Miss Opal's diagnosis, Miss Opal became adamant.

"Get your ass in gear and get the nurse," she said. "She's having a stroke."

Shortly thereafter, an ambulance arrived at the nursing home. And a stroke victim was on her way to the hospital.

Dr. Dick's 50-Year Deal

While the Clinton Infirmary was a lifesaver for people throughout the area, it wasn't the only place in town where you could get medical care.

Dr. R. K. "Dick" Munson had his own office near downtown. If his patients required hospitalization, he would send them to Centreville, Miss.

When I was attending LSU, Dr. Dick became my primary physician. I thought he was a great diagnostician, but he didn't hesitate to seek more specialized help when necessary.

My classmate, Claude Rouchon, could vouch for that.

Claude spent the summer between his junior and senior years living in Baton Rouge with his aunt and uncle. He worked out with LSU football players at a health club in preparation for his final high school season. He also had a job.

Claude was working when he first noticed something was wrong.

A woman customer at the National Food store asked him to carry two watermelons to her car. He couldn't do it. He had to carry them one at a time.

Claude first thought he had been working out too much. But he became weaker and weaker – until he couldn't execute the simplest task. And he surely couldn't play football.

Doctors couldn't figure out what was wrong. He was even advised to see a psychiatrist.

"Doctor Dick was the only one who didn't give up on me," Claude said. "Everybody else gave up on me."

Dr. Dick told Claude he knew a doctor at Ochsner Medical Center in New Orleans who possibly could help him. He phoned the doctor ahead of time and briefed him on Claude's condition.

After Claude was tested and observed by doctors at Ochsner, they determined he had Myasthenia Gravis.

"Doctor Dick saved my life," Claude said.

Dr. Dick Munson served Clinton for more than 50 years.

He couldn't save everybody's life. But he tried. And his effort was the foundation of his 52-year practice.

"I remember him telling me who his first patient was," Dr. Dick's daughter, Kay, said. "Her name was Emma Dunn. She had a small infant who was just several weeks old. She had been told her baby wasn't going to live."

As soon as Dr. Dick saw the baby, he called deputy Albert Moffit at the jail.

"Bring your cop car to the office," Dr. Dick said.

He put Emma Dunn's dying child in the back seat of Mr. Moffit's car and said, "Take the child to Big Charity (hospital) in New Orleans. And don't stop for anything."

The baby didn't live. But word spread about the baby's doctor: "Doctor Dick would go the extra mile."

Dr. Dick's family knew all about that.

People came to their home requesting emergency care. Often that meant delivering a baby.

Miss Katherine, Dr. Dick's wife, was concerned about being left at home with her two young children, Maureen and Kay, at night, so the whole family would make the house call en masse.

"Sometimes, we would go way out in the country into no man's land," Kay remembered.

No man's land couldn't always be reached in their Plymouth. Instead, someone might come from the house in a horse and buggy and take Dr. Dick to the patient.

Miss Katherine had Kay and Maureen lie down on the back seat, although sleep was virtually impossible in the summer.

"We would try to sleep, and mosquitoes would eat us alive," Kay said.

Their mother combatted the mosquitoes with cigarette smoke. Second-hand smoke probably never served a better purpose.

"It was all of the time," Kay said. "In his beginning years of practice, that's what he did. He would make house calls and deliver babies. Some nights, it was more than one."

People didn't need a medical excuse to visit the Munsons. Sometimes, friends would drop by in the morning seeking advice from Dr. Dick on other matters.

"I can remember people coming up to the house before school," Kay said. "They would sit at the kitchen table and ask him different things. In those days, your doctor was part of your family."

The entire family became immersed in Dr. Dick's practice. Miss Katherine initially kept the books. Maureen and Kay did them later.

Dr. Dick managed his office's finances just as he practiced medicine. He did it his way.

"Daddy had his mind made up from the beginning," Kay said. "He never turned it over twice in his mind. He wasn't going to take money from the government.

"He said, 'I will not sell my soul to the government. If I take money from the government, it's just a matter of time before they tell me what to do.' "

And you didn't tell Dr. Dick what to do.

His payment was based on an honor system of sorts. If a patient couldn't pay, Dr. Dick only asked that the patient pay when he could. Some never paid at all. But he didn't want to know which patients paid or didn't pay. He saw them as patients, not sources of revenue.

Someone once contacted Dr. Dick, offering his services as a bill collector. That didn't go well.

"When he got through with him on the phone, we never again heard from anyone offering to be a bill collector," Kay said.

Dr. Dick would log into a ledger what he did for a patient. Miss Katherine would transcribe the posts into a leather-bound ledger. Miss Katherine, Kay, or Maureen would type the bills.

And then, the patient might or might not pay them.

Myrtle Hall was Dr. Dick's longtime nurse, and Gladys Palmer also worked in his office. But he was truly hands-on when it came to his patients.

He took their blood pressure. He listened to their hearts. He observed. And he remembered.

Bill Ourso, my high school principal, was a longtime patient of Dr. Dick's. When Mr. Ourso had a problem with his heart, Dr. Dick was the first to know.

And he knew without a heart catheter or stress test. He knew by listening.

"I had listened to his heart for decades," he told Kay. "When I put that stethoscope on him, I knew it had changed."

Dr. Dick didn't always go by the book. And sometimes, he had his own book.

"He never drew blood to check somebody's thyroid," Kay said. "He had this little book with a wheel that would line up information – including blood pressure, height, male or female – and give someone the standing of their thyroid.

"I never understood the chart. It was very complex. But it worked."

Dr. Dick knew he wanted to practice medicine from a young age. He often spent his summers in Pascagoula, Miss., where his grandfather, Dr. William Richard Kell, was a prominent physician. His grandfather stressed the importance of using all your senses in studying your patients.

Dr. Edgar Hull, one of Dr. Dick's instructors at LSU Medical School, was a friend of Dr. Kell's. He reinforced his friend's medical philosophy.

"You have to smell, you have to touch, you've got to feel things," he told his students.

Dr. Dick took all that to heart and later applied it in his own practice. That practice revolved around his patients.

After seeing his morning patients, Dr. Dick would return home for lunch, then take a 30- to 45-minute nap.

"He wanted to be clear-headed for his afternoon patients," Kay said. "He thought that was the best way to do it."

His afternoon schedule varied according to his patient load. Patients didn't see him by appointment. They came to his office and waited. Sometimes, he might not see his last patient until 7 p.m.

Medicine was first and foremost with Dr. Dick, but he had a wide range of other interests. He raised a variety of camellias, collected gold and silver coins, hunted turkeys, and loved horse racing. He also developed a passion for opera while attending Tulane. And he was one of Clinton High's biggest football fans.

Dr. Dick was a quarterback on Clinton's six-man football team in 1940 and later became a longtime physician for the Clinton Eagles.

"Other than when he was in the Korean War for two years, I don't know of him missing a Friday night football game," Kay said.

Even when Dr. Dick was in Korea, he would write letters home to encourage the team.

Before he left Clinton to fulfill his military obligation, Dr. Dick served the football team as more than a doctor. He also was the public-address announcer.

Just as Dr. Dick had his own way of practicing medicine, he also had a distinct style as the voice of the Clinton Eagles. He seemed more like a radio play-by-play broadcaster than a public-address announcer. And he was anything but objective.

The Eagles were fine with that.

At the end of one season when he was stationed in Korea, they formally commended him for his devotion to the program.

"His work on the microphone during the playing of each game was out of this world," their commendation read. "He was totally partial, and deliberately so, and could take a very ordinary ball game and work the hometown fans into a frenzy of excitement."

Opposing schools weren't as impressed with Dr. Dick's announcing.

"All of the opponents hated him," Kay said. "They said he was nothing but a cheerleader on the microphone.

"One time, it was either Greensburg or Kentwood, the other team called and said, 'If he announces, we're not coming.' "

She didn't remember how that turned out. But my guess is Dr. Dick's sidekick, Johnny Barnett, stepped in as a substitute.

Mr. Johnny was beside Dr. Dick at every game – just in case. If Dr. Dick received an emergency medical call, Mr. Johnny would take over the announcing. And when he gave Dr. Dick a break, I don't remember him being any less of a homer.

But they occasionally could be critical of the home team. You just never heard that over the public-address system. While keeping stats, I usually was within earshot of them on the sideline as we followed the game from one goal line to the other. Once the microphone was off, they didn't mind expressing their frustration with the team or an individual player.

Thanks to Dr. Dick and Mr. Johnny, I felt as though I had the best seat in the house.

Dr. Dick stood the test of time as both an announcer and a doctor. When he finally retired at 75, someone asked why he practiced for 52 years.

"When I started practicing medicine, I said if God let's me live, I will give the town 50 years," Dr. Dick said. "And I went to Korea for two years."

He might have practiced even longer if he hadn't set such high standards for himself. Although he kept meticulous records on each patient, Dr. Dick didn't have to check them. He remembered.

"He didn't ask me what antibiotic he gave a patient," said Kay, who worked as his assistant in the final years of his practice. "He would tell me.

"Toward the end, it would frustrate him to death because he would have to look at the ledger. 'This is disgraceful, I have to come in here and look,' he would say.

"So, he knew when his time was up."

His retirement also marked the end of an era.

The next time you visit a general doctor, he's apt to be looking at a computer while you're describing your symptoms.

Diagnosing a medical malady is difficult under any circumstances. My friend, Mike Felps, a former hospital business manager, once told me, "If you walk into a hospital with a spear sticking in your chest, they can tell you what your problem is. Otherwise, it's a guessing game."

But I would have taken Dr. Dick's best guess over just about anybody's, because when I was in his office, I always thought I had his undivided attention. He wasn't perfunctorily going through the motions. He was using all his senses.

And if he couldn't solve your problem, he would do his best – as Claude and Emma Dunn could attest - to find somebody who could. His practice began with his trying to save Emma Dunn's baby. He was still treating her and her family when she died.

"Emma died a few months before Daddy," Kay said. "Her funeral was the last one he attended."

Before Dr. Dick died, he expressed regret about retiring. His patients also had regrets about that.

Kay remembers one of them saying, "No one has controlled my thyroid since your daddy died."

Clinton's Invisible Runner

It was a Friday morning in December, the eighth grade, and I had an upstairs window seat for Louisiana History at Clinton High School. My right leg was twitching to the rain, which had been falling on and off all week.

What do I remember about Louisiana History? Bienville, the Longs (Earl and Huey) … and my teacher, Genevieve Williams, whose intellect and teaching skills probably were wasted on us. That's about it.

But I remember that Friday in December 1961. I remember the rain couldn't end soon enough, and nightfall couldn't come fast enough. Clinton was playing for a state championship in football on its home field.

I had attended the 1959 Sugar Bowl in which LSU defeated Clemson 7-0 to complete an unbeaten, national championship season. But I hadn't attended any other sporting event of greater magnitude than the Class B state championship game between Clinton and Oberlin.

Class B was the smallest of the state's four classifications. Clinton usually fielded a good team – good enough to sometimes beat Class A and AA teams in non-district games – while competing successfully in a district that included surrounding towns like Zachary, Greensburg, Jackson, St. Francisville, and Kentwood.

I wasn't old enough to have appreciated Clinton's first state championship in 1950. However, in 1961, I was a more seasoned fan, quite capable of comprehending the significance of pulling for the best team in the state. In fact, I was practically part of the program.

Chuck Charlet and I had worked as ushers throughout the regular season. A mindless job? Not hardly. Even now, I can remember that we booted 35 people from reserved seating. We executed our routine as well as the Clinton Eagles ran their split-T offense.

"Excuse me, could we see your reserved ticket?" was our opening line. We took turns saying it with amazing consistency, knowing the answer before we asked. We knew who belonged in the reserved section, so there was a surge of adrenaline anytime an intruder took a seat in "our section."

We made sure they took a seat and got settled. Only then would we make our move, faking politeness and concealing our elation as we informed them why they would have to find a different seat. As they walked away, I added them to our seasonal total.

But there was no ushering to be done at the state championship. I was just a fan, well aware that more than a state championship was at stake. It also would be George Haynes' last game as a Clinton Eagle.

Clinton had a history of good running backs. Billy Ray Curtis, Francis Hunt, and Bubby Jackson – to name a few. George's older brother, Charles Frank, was another. But Clinton had never seen anyone like George. He wasn't just one of Clinton's best running backs. He was one of the best running backs in the country.

And this would be his last high school game.

George was born in Centreville, Miss., and lived his first years in Norwood, which was then a sawmill town just across the state line in Louisiana. His family moved to Clinton when he was 4.

He was in the sixth grade when he started working out. George doesn't even remember how the workouts came about. But every day, he would run sprints and jump rope.

"I just wanted it real bad," he said. "I don't know why."

His mother, Eula Lee, wasn't thrilled about him jumping rope in the living room, but his father, Frank, insisted, "If that boy wants to work out, let him do it."

George didn't play football until the seventh grade. By then, he already was exceling in another sport - swimming. He didn't think of it so much as a sport, as summer recreation.

"In the summer, we would go swimming in some creek every day." he said.

Swimming might have been common for George and his friends. Swimming like George wasn't common. After he began swimming competitively in Clinton and other nearby towns, he never lost a race.

When he was 15, his father entered him in every age bracket of a meet: 14-15, 16-17, 18-19 and 19-20. George proceeded to win the freestyle and breast stroke in every age class.

They left without the trophies, though. "You don't need them," George's father said.

"I'm sure he would have let me take the trophies if I had insisted," George said.

But as good as George was in swimming, football came first by the time he reached the seventh grade. Two years later, he was good enough to start on the varsity as a freshman. By the 10th grade, he was getting letters from colleges throughout the country.

In 1959, No. 1 LSU and No. 2 Ole Miss – both unbeaten – met in Tiger Stadium in what is now regarded as one of the greatest games in college football history. It was decided in LSU's favor, 7-3, when eventual Heisman Trophy winner Billy Cannon ran through or past half the Ole Miss defense on an 89-yard, fourth-quarter punt return for a touchdown – then led a game-saving goal-line stand on Ole Miss' last possession.

George watched the game from the Ole Miss bench as a special guest of coach Johnny Vaught, who gave him a huge allotment of tickets for George's family and friends. That's how badly Ole Miss wanted to sign him.

Ole Miss wasn't alone. College football's most prominent programs, including Notre Dame, were aware of George.

But you didn't have to be a college recruiter to know about George. By his senior year, fans from Baton Rouge and small towns throughout the area would come to Clinton to watch George play.

No one carried the ball better for the Clinton Eagles than George Haynes.

Who could blame them? At 6-1, 190 pounds, he was bigger than many of the linemen on his team, and one of the top sprinters in the state, having already broken the 10-second mark in the 100-yard dash.

You could get a sense of George's power, as well as his speed, in track. Ted Chaney, who was a team manager, got an up-close view of that.

One of Ted's jobs was to provide additional support to George's starting blocks, which then were affixed to the track with spikes on each side. The apparatus was sufficient for most runners, but not George.

"His takeoff and push-back were so tremendous, he would tear the blocks out of the ground," said Ted, who stood on the metal plate to the side of the blocks for additional support.

Too bad that anyone who tried to tackle George couldn't have seen him come out of the blocks. Then, they would have known what they were up against. On second thought, perhaps it was just as well they didn't know

Aside from watching Pistol Pete Maravich play basketball during my college days at LSU, I never enjoyed watching an athlete more than George. He could run over or around defenders, and he often made it look easy.

Once, in a tough game against St. Francisville, a punted ball had almost rolled to a stop when several opposing players gathered around it. Then, just before the ball came to rest, George swooped in, scooped it up, and took off on another touchdown run.

Charles Henry Andrews, who was a year older than George, was an outstanding football player at Clinton and went on to play college ball as well. Like others who played with and against George, he marveled at his running ability.

"I played with some good ones at Southeastern (Louisiana) and LSU," he said. "But George was the best I ever played with."

My friend, Mike Felps, concurred. Mike was so big for his age that he was on the varsity team as an eighth grader, when George was a senior. I asked him what it was like trying to tackle George in practice.

"He was invisible," Mike said.

Clinton's Billy Andrews, an NFL linebacker for 11 seasons, said, "If he hadn't gotten hurt, he would have been in the NFL in my opinion."

The combination of speed and power wasn't the only reason so many colleges were interested in George. He also was a fierce competitor.

"When he had the ball in his hands, he would knock your butt off," said Johnny Beauchamp, who started in Clinton's defensive line. "One time in practice, they ran an end sweep. When I went up to tackle him, he butted me in the chest with his head. I was out a week."

Against Liberty, George lost one of his contact lenses. He asked coach Hubert Polk if someone would put tape over that eye, so he would be able to see well enough to return punts. Coach Polk didn't go for his suggestion, but George stayed in the game as a running back.

Johnny, who was a year behind George in school, was so impressed with him that he chose George as the subject of an English essay. He's still upset that he only got a "C" on the paper.

Opponents were just as impressed. In a playoff game against Patterson, George scored all 43 of Clinton's points. But the game against Kentwood his senior year is the one I remember the most. Coach Hubert Polk would empty the bench in trying to hold down the score, which finally reached 80-0.

Mercifully for Kentwood, George played only one quarter. He got the ball four times and scored four touchdowns. I'm convinced he could have rushed for 700 yards if he had played the entire game.

The competition would be altogether different in the state championship game. Oberlin was the preseason pick to win the state championship. And it only had to run on the field to make you realize why. Its players were huge compared to Clinton's. As if Oberlin needed another advantage, the rain had provided it.

"It seemed like it had rained a week straight," George said. "I couldn't believe how much standing water there was. We couldn't even practice much. We went to the gym and got some things done."

As the Clinton cheerleaders decorated the goal posts before the game, Kay Munson remembers seeing the Oberlin team bus arrive at the stadium.

"One of the first players that got off the bus was (running back) Hoyle Granger," Kay said. "His blue jeans were cut down both outer seams and they were laced with leather. His legs were so big they couldn't fit in those jeans. He was a freak."

On a soggy field against a much bigger team, Clinton was overwhelmed. Would-be-tacklers repeatedly slid off Oberlin's 215-pound running back.

George still managed to give us one more highlight. After Oberlin had taken a 7-0 lead, George took a screen pass and ran for a touchdown. Like so many of the best running backs, he had the ability to change speeds without slowing down. That play reminded you why LSU coach Paul Dietzel and defensive coordinator Charlie McClendon were at the game.

George's last highlight was also Clinton's last gasp. Oberlin won 34-13, and Clinton had to wait another year to win its second state championship.

But the state championship loss wouldn't be George's last or greatest disappointment.

George liked both Ole Miss and LSU, but his official visit to Ole Miss would have the greatest impact on his overall recruitment. He and two other recruits were aboard a twin-engine plane, which was supposed to land at Baton Rouge's Ryan Airport on the return trip. They were close to their landing spot when the propellers went out.

"What was going on?" George thought. "I looked at the pilot. He had sweat the size of a nickel rolling off his head. 'We've got to find a place to land,' he said.

"We went right over this guy's house. He threw his coffee cup down. We did about two turns before we landed in a field. It all happened so fast."

The plane landed safely, but George looked at recruiting differently after that.

"I was planning to take a trip to Notre Dame and Oklahoma," he said. "But after going through that, I didn't want to get on a plane anymore."

His decision really came down to Ole Miss and LSU. And since Charles Frank was about to get a scholarship after walking on at LSU, George thought about his parents not being able to see both sons play if he went to Ole Miss. So, he signed with LSU.

Although George was Clinton's featured running back as a fullback in the "T," his skills were ideally suited for tailback in LSU's I-formation. Freshmen didn't play on the varsity then, but in 1963 as a sophomore, George might have been LSU's starting tailback if he hadn't suffered a hamstring injury.

Joe Labruzzo won the starting job while George tried to get healthy. I'm sure all of Clinton was disappointed. I know I was. So was my former ushering colleague.

In an early-season at Tiger Stadium, when Labruzzo went down briefly with an injury, Chuck screamed from his seat: "Get that bum off the field and put Haynes in.' The fans around us glared. Labruzzo, a small but tough running back from South Louisiana, already had become a crowd favorite. But not our favorite. Chuck repeated his yell just to make sure everyone near us understood our allegiance.

George had come back from injuries before. As a high school junior, he injured his pelvis and tore his groin muscle, putting him out for the year and sabotaging Clinton's shot for a state championship.

His worst injury was yet to come.

When George returned from the hamstring injury, his first game was against Ole Miss on national television. He remembers taking a hard hit to a shoulder that knocked him off balance. Just as his cleats stuck in the ground, two Ole Miss players hit him simultaneously. An Achilles tendon was shredded on impact.

His season ended, and a medical nightmare began.

The injured leg became infected during surgery. Two more surgeries were required to clean out the wound. The leg turned black, and doctors feared he could lose it.

He didn't lose the leg. But he lost something else.

George was on crutches for two years. Doctors told him he would be lucky if he could walk. But he not only walked, he returned to football.

His coaches were skeptical. "George, you'll get it all torn up again," they warned him.

"I think I can play," George said.

So, they gave him a chance. He still had speed but couldn't push off with the same power. He was switched from running back to wide receiver, where he started as a senior.

I didn't like watching him play after that. Here was this star running back being reduced to a role player, a wide receiver on a team that rarely threw the ball.

"Sometimes, I think I was stupid (for making the comeback)," he said. "But when you play ball, you just don't want to give up.

"You see athletes who don't know when to quit. I can understand that. I didn't know when to quit."

But George believes that same determination helped him become a successful businessman in Baton Rouge.

"Things clicked (in business)," he said. "That's one thing football teaches you. You gotta get up and go again. You can't give up."

He didn't give up. But football gave up on him.

Before the injury, before he played his first down as a college running back, George already was getting letters from NFL teams. After the Achilles injury, he never heard from them again.

Oberlin's Granger went on to star at Mississippi State and later was a running back with the Houston Oilers. Clinton won the state championship the year after George graduated. And Andrews, the 162-pound linebacker and center on that championship team, just kept getting bigger and better until he became a starting linebacker for the Cleveland Browns.

But when I think back to Friday night football at Clinton High School, I think more about George – the running back my friend, Mike, described as "invisible," and that Kentwood couldn't tackle. I also think about all the people who came to Clinton for no other reason but to watch George Haynes play. And I think all of them must have been as disappointed as I was, when injuries took away a football career that was just getting started.

"You had those dreams," George said. "You're almost there, and then it gets yanked away from you.

"You feel like you got cheated a little.

"But you've got to live with it and move on."

The Touchdown Nobody Saw

When Clinton played Erath in the 1962 Class B state football semifinals, I rode the "Lily White" bus to the game.

Color had nothing to do with the nickname. It was dubbed the "Lily White" because its passengers presumably didn't take their football with a strong dose of alcohol.

But it wasn't the only chartered bus to transport Eagles fans from Clinton to Erath. The other one was named the "Mogen David."

I'm not suggesting that everyone who rode the "Mogen David" was a hard drinker, but it was safe to say they weren't teetotalers. And if you were going to name a bus after an alcoholic beverage, Mogen David was as good as any. Songwriters would back me up on that.

"Will they have Mogen David in Heaven?" the Gatlin Brothers asked in song. Brenda Lee sang, "I was Mogen David wine, he was Chablis '59."

"Lily White" has been mentioned in songs, too. But if you're riding a bus with that name, you're less apt to burst out in song than if you're aboard the Mogen David.

My mother bought me a ticket on the Lily White, which seemed like the prudent choice. But buses sometimes are like games. They don't turn out as expected.

Our bus wrecked.

No one was seriously injured, but I remember being jostled around when the Lily White ran off the road. The driver probably veered off the road when he couldn't see through the heavy fog that was gathering in South Louisiana that Friday night. However, we still made it to the game on time, and no doubt provided a comical sidebar to the Mogen David bunch, whose bus held the road for the entire trip.

Our mishap added another twist to one of the most bizarre games I've ever seen. In fact, I didn't see part it. Neither did anyone else.

You could have painted the football neon green, and fans still wouldn't have been able to follow it consistently. It's as though the first half of the game was played behind a curtain. The fog was as thick as the Cajun accents in Erath.

"When we lined up on the kickoff, you could see the feet of the front line of blockers, but you couldn't see anything else," Clinton linebacker Billy Andrews said. "And you couldn't see where the ball went."

Other than the ball, the hardest thing to see was Stuart Chaney, Clinton's junior running back. He was powerful for his size and the quickest player on a team known for its quickness. Sometimes, on a straight dive play, the quarterback practically would have to lunge toward Stuart to make the handoff in time.

Former Clinton high school All-American running back George Haynes was big and fast. But as a sophomore, Stuart could keep up with him for the first half of a 100-yard dash.

Stuart was more than quick against Erath, whose players probably still discuss at every class reunion how the Clinton running back ended up in their end zone.

His first-half touchdown run of about 50 yards came on the most basic play in coach Hubert Polk's offense. But the "quick dive" over right tackle must have seemed like a trick play to Erath.

"Nobody knew he scored," Billy said. "Nobody on the field or in the stands. The official came back with his hands up."

Said Clinton lineman Johnny Beauchamp: "Everybody got up from where we were blocking and couldn't find the ball. Then, here comes this referee from the end zone and got us to do the extra point."

The fog began to clear in the second half, but Erath never did find the end zone.

Clinton won the game 12-0 and beat St. Edmund's of Eunice the following week to win the school's second state championship in football.

A year later, Clinton made the playoffs for a third consecutive season and likely would have advanced further if not for injury. Stuart suffered a season-ending knee injury in the first game, and Clinton was forced to play the rest of the season without its best player.

Injuries almost sabotaged Clinton's state championship season, too.

Eagles quarterback Amile deGeneres injured his knee late in the regular season against Ferriday, which handed Clinton its only loss of the season. Some fans didn't handle the defeat well.

Ferriday's Ronnie Jeter, a bowling ball of an all-state fullback, was exiting the field when Clinton's Norman Johnson and Teddy Lloyd confronted him. According to witnesses, Norman fared even worse than the Eagles. Jeter whacked him in the face with his helmet and kept walking.

Norman got a nickname out of it, though. "Cyclone Johnson," Johnny called him.

Johnny was a regular cyclone himself in the middle of Clinton's line for much of the state championship season. Hardly a game went by that he wasn't flagged for a personal foul penalty. "Or maybe, two," Billy pointed out.

Johnny's penalty was more severe against Amite.

After Billy intercepted a pass, he encountered what Johnny deemed an unnecessary hit out of bounds from an Amite player.

"He piled on Billy," Johnny said. "Hit him in the back. Then, he kind of flipped over and came up on his knees. When he did, I took him out. I wasn't going to have that."

Neither were the officials. They kicked Johnny out of the game.

Johnny's competitive nature didn't change at the University of Arkansas at Monticello. He was one of the six Clinton seniors off the state championship team who went on to play college football.

Monticello was winning a game handily when an opposing punt returner was racing down the sideline on his way to a touchdown. That's when Johnny intervened.

"He already had run one back for a touchdown," Johnny said. "But we were beating the devil out of them.

"I was standing on the sideline, and just stuck out my foot. He tried to stop, slipped and fell down."

Johnny quickly removed his foot from the field.

"The referees didn't know what happened," he said. "They didn't know who did what."

But they knew enough to penalize Johnny's team.

Clinton fans would have expected no less from Johnny, whose late hits were even put to music before he graduated.

In the spring following Clinton's 1962 state championship season, the team was honored on "Eagle Day." The 1950 state champs were included in the festivities, which featured a flag football game between the two state championship teams.

The celebration also included songs that fourth-grade teacher Bernadotte Phares wrote about Clinton's three all-state players: Billy, Amile and Johnny.

Johnny's lyrics were the most appropriate: "Oh, Johnny, you were so rough; oh, Johnny you were so tough. … And the whistle would blow and it would be … "

The student body took the cue and shouted in unison: "15 yards!"

Johnny had another penalty coming before he graduated. So did his teammates, Billy and running back/linebacker J.D. Gardner. They were expelled from school for three days, though they were still allowed to take part in Eagle Day.

"When the bell rang for us to go to Miss Sue's home room, we dropped cracker balls as we went up the steps," Billy said.

Other students did the rest, stepping on the cracker balls and producing one pop after another. Unfortunately, teacher Cecil Richardson supposedly tripped on one of the cracker balls. Although she was uninjured, the incident became more serious with her misstep.

When the students assembled in the school auditorium, coach Hubert Polk said no one was leaving until he got a confession.

"We agreed that all the football team would say we did it," Billy said.

The strength-in-numbers strategy probably seemed like a good idea at the time, but it didn't work out as planned. Billy, Johnny and J. D. raised their hands as an admission of guilt. Nobody else followed suit, proving that teamwork - even on a state championship team - only goes so far.

"I thought this would be fun and games," Billy said. "When I got home, it was not fun and games. Daddy worked me hard. He didn't even let me come to town.

"They did let us come back and get our awards. And they let us play in the flag football game."

Billy didn't remember the score of the flag game. He did remember that teammate Jerry Rouchon bloodied the nose of one of the 1950 state champions.

That's hardly surprising. Clinton didn't win its 1962 championship on finesse. And it made up for its lack of size with toughness and togetherness.

"The team agreed if you smoked or drank, we were going to kick your tail," Billy said. "After we lost in our junior season, we committed that we would win the state championship. We believed we would win the state championship no matter what.

That belief might not have been shared outside the locker room. Clinton couldn't win a state championship with a high school All-American running back in 1961. And it couldn't win in 1960 when George was a junior and its line was bigger than some college lines. So, how would it win with an under-sized team lacking in star power?

But the 1962 team had an uncommon desire for winning – and to each other.

"Some teams just click," said Ben Dart, who was a sophomore tackle on the state championship team. "And that one clicked. They were like brothers."

Sometimes, their camaraderie was evident on film.

On one goal-line play late in a game, Johnny admitted he was too tired to pull and make a block. So, Billy pulled from his center position and made the block.

Coach Polk didn't know how the play unfolded until he reviewed the film.

As determined as the team was to win a championship, it still had lapses. After all, we're talking about teenagers here.

That's where Coach Polk came in.

Ted Chaney, who was a team manager, remembers a game Clinton was winning with ease but failing to please its head coach.

"He turned around on the sideline and told (assistant coach Sid White), 'They're goofing off. And they're going to pay for it Monday. I'm going to make them run wind sprints till they fall flat on their face.'

"Then, he spots me and here he comes. He gets right in my face and says, 'You managers are going to run, too.' "

Johnny remembers another game in which Coach Polk wasn't happy before it started.

"It was our homecoming game against Greensburg," Johnny said. "He said homecoming was for the girls and fans. But 'If you don't get out there and perform, there won't be a homecoming for you. You will be practicing.'

"We beat the crap out of them."

In fact, it was a tough game for anyone not wearing a Clinton uniform. An official realized that on a screen pass, which left J.D. running for a touchdown behind a convoy of blockers, one of whom was Johnny.

"I saw somebody that didn't have the same colored uniform as us coming up out of the corner of my eye," Johnny said. "I took him out."

He took out an official.

"I went up to him and apologized," Johnny said. "But he said it was his fault for getting up too close."

You didn't have to watch a game to appreciate the team's affinity for contact.

"Whatever drills we did in practice, we were wide open," Johnny said. "We practiced like we played."

The team's underclassmen could attest to that.

"I was just holding dummies for those guys," said Ben Dart, who was a sophomore tackle on the state championship team. "I was getting run over. Those guys whipped up on us.

"They were tough. But they made us tougher. And I got a state championship jacket, too."

Claude Rouchon, who was a freshman lineman on the championship team, remembers how demanding the practices could be.

His brother, Jerry, was a senior and another tough customer in the line. But that didn't help Claude any.

"Coach Polk never let my brother hit me," Claude said. "But Billy, Johnny, and everybody else hit me."

Sometimes, when Claude and the other younger players were holding a dummy for the veterans, "they would block the dummy and try to hit you with a forearm," Claude said. "Just to keep you on your toes."

As devoted as the team was to hitting in practice, it didn't have the same zeal for non-contact drills.

"A visiting coach came by to borrow some film from Coach Polk," Johnny said. "I was in the dressing room, so I heard Coach Polk tell him, 'This is the most miserable bunch I've tried to coach. If they're not beating up on each other, the practices are horrible.' "

So, Clinton hit hard in practice and games. And got away with it for the most part.

But the injury to Amile was a shocker. He was one of Clinton's all-time best athletes – a state champion pole vaulter and an outstanding two-way player in football as a defensive back and quarterback.

"He was our best hitter and our best offensive player," Billy said. "That would have thrown off a normal team. But Ricky Callicutt kind of carried us through."

Ricky, who already started at safety on defense, shared the quarterbacking duties in the state championship game with Amile, who couldn't run with his usual effectiveness because of the knee injury.

It was just another example of how the team tightened its ranks amid adversity. And how driven it was to finish what the previous team started.

But this time, there would be no Oberlin and Hoyle Granger looming at the finish line.

He's Gonna Eat

Billy Andrews decided at the age of 9 that he would play pro football. When he informed his parents, Charles Rist and Doodle Andrews, of his intentions, they probably smiled in agreement.

After all, anything seems possible when you're that age. And far be it from good parents to discourage a childhood dream.

I was feeling pretty good about sports at that age myself. Not that I imagined myself playing in the NFL. But I did have a "magical tiger" that I believed could influence the outcome of football games.

This wasn't just some kid's fantasy. It was a fact. And I had a track record to prove it.

Whenever LSU fell behind in a game, I would take my stuffed tiger off the lower shelf of my closet and bring him into the room where Mother and I were listening to the game.

I instituted this strategy during the 1958 season, unaware of where it might lead. LSU won every game on the way to a national championship, which meant that my tiger also was unbeaten.

The 1959 season didn't unfold much differently from the previous season. Both the Tigers and my tiger were unbeaten through the first seven games.

Then, something strange happened.

When LSU fell behind an underdog Tennessee team in the fourth quarter, I fetched my tiger from the closet, positioned him next to the radio and waited for his mystical powers to impact a sporting event that was taking place more than 600 miles away in Knoxville, Tenn.

But this time, the momentum didn't change. Tennessee thwarted LSU's two-point conversion attempt following a final touchdown and held on for a 14-13 victory.

LSU football was never the same for me after that. My relationship with the stuffed tiger changed, too. He never joined me for another game, which probably was just fine with Mother, who might have become concerned if I had gone from 11 to 12 still believing that a small, stuffed tiger with crooked ears was capable of anything other than remaining still.

The tiger subsequently was moved from the bottom to the top shelf of the closet and then to a toy chest on the back porch – until, like other childhood toys, he finally just went away.

Billy's sports fantasy had more staying power.

He started lifting weights at Alvin Roy's health club in Baton Rouge when he was 12. That was a means to an end. If he were going to play in the NFL, he would need to get bigger and stronger.

He did get stronger. He got stronger still by lifting bales of hay with his brother Charles Henry on their father's farm.

As the barbells and hay piled up behind him, Billy imagined himself moving ever closer to the NFL – even if no one else did.

Sometimes, before Miss Doodle and Mr. Charles Rist went to sleep they would wonder about Billy.

They didn't want to bash his dream, but they also considered the harm in allowing him to pursue what seemed like an unrealistic goal.

"We didn't want to discourage you," Miss Doodle told Billy many years later. "We knew you weren't going to play pro football. But we just decided to act like you were gonna play."

Humor the kid, right? Soon enough, he would realize for himself that he was too small and too slow to play in the NFL. Then, he would put aside his childhood fantasy – just as I did my stuffed tiger – and get on with his life.

Instead, Billy got on with his dream. He kept working on the farm and working out at the health club. By the eighth grade, he was already 6-feet-1 – as tall as he would ever be. As strong as he was for his size, he looked nothing like a future pro.

Lack of size was an issue for Billy from the beginning. He was born six weeks premature and only weighed 3 pounds.

But he was determined to overcome that once he began pursuing a pro football career at a young age.

"I drank a gallon of milk every day," he said. "I also drank a glass of cream."

His daily diet included a mixture of cream, milk, six raw eggs, sugar and vanilla extract. All of that was topped off with as much ice cream that would fit into a blender. He drank three of those concoctions a day.

"When I was younger, I wouldn't gain weight," he said. "I was allergic to everything and had stomach problems."

Nonetheless, he was still big enough to be a Clinton Eagle. And he jumped at any opportunity to prove himself, even when surrounded by more seasoned players.

Veteran players were going head-to-head in individual drills one practice when coach Hubert Polk shouted, "Give me another man in here."

Billy was the first to volunteer.

"I said, 'Give me a man in here,' " Coach Polk said. "I don't need a boy."

"I was so mad I was crying in front of the guys," Billy said. "That made me even madder. I loved Coach Polk, but I said, 'I'm gonna show him. I'm gonna be the man he needs.' "

When starting center and linebacker Ed Freeman was injured, Billy became a starter as a sophomore. But after Ed was healthy enough to return at center, Billy held a starting position at linebacker.

By Billy's junior year, when he helped Clinton reach the state championship game, he still weighed only 153 pounds. But he was gaining motivation, if not weight.

Clinton's Billy Andrews running for a game-winning touchdown on the first "Monday Night Football" game.

"My junior year, I believe everybody on our starting team but me made first-, second-, or third-team all-district," Billy said.

Coach Polk knew Billy wouldn't take that well. So, he wanted to break the news to him. He went to Billy's house and told him that Billy and a player from Pine Grove had tied for first-team center. Since the Pine Grove player was a senior, the coaches decided to make him first team.

But instead of dropping Billy to the second team, the coaches "got to politicking," Coach Polk said. And Billy was left out altogether.

That ended up working to Billy's advantage.

He asked Coach Polk if he could take the practice dummies and one-man sleds to his house that off- season. He was committed to working even harder.

And he remained as coachable as ever.

"If Coach Polk told me to step with my right foot, I stepped with my right foot," Billy said. "If he said take it on with your left shoulder, I took it on with my left shoulder."

More and more, he also demonstrated an obvious knack for the game. Linebackers need strength to take on blockers and ball carriers. They need speed and quickness to cover backs in the passing game. But as much as any position on the field, linebacking requires intuitiveness. And Billy just had a sense for playing the position.

"I could read the play and be gone before anybody else had diagnosed it," Billy said.

Johnny Beauchamp, a defensive lineman on Clinton's state championship team, remembered how Billy could decipher a play just by an opponent's alignment.

"Billy really studied the scouting report and remembered it," Johnny said. "When they lined up, he could tell us what hole they were running at. I don't know how he read it that well, but he was right about every time."

You can imagine the effect it had on an opponent for Billy to be calling out where its play was headed as if he had been in the offensive huddle.

"They were plum baffled by it," Johnny said.

Although Billy's size might have been a problem for college recruiters, no one could ignore how well he understood the game, and that was as much of an asset as speed or size.

Southeastern coach Stanley Galloway offered Billy a scholarship two weeks before the signing date. "We're just going to postdate this," he told Billy.

Just like that, Billy was assured of playing college football. He was a step closer to the NFL.

Billy got LSU's attention after he intercepted two passes in Clinton's victory over St. Edmund's of Eunice in the Class B state championship game and again in the Louisiana High School All-Star game when he played both offense and defense.

But when LSU assistant coach John North offered him a scholarship, Billy said, "My dad said if I signed with Southeastern, I was done. You said I was too small. I'm still too small."

He was getting bigger, though. By the summer before his first college season, he was up to 185 pounds. He also had gained speed.

And he had gotten married. Kay Munson left Clinton after her junior year of high school, married Billy, and moved with him to Hammond. She soon realized how serious he was about becoming a pro football player, and that his goal would take a commitment on her part, too.

"I will eat," he told her after they were married.

She laughs at that now, but it was no laughing matter for a young wife who couldn't cook. Kay returned to Clinton for a cram course in cooking, as taught by the Munson family maid, Margaret Sensley.

"Red beans and rice, roast and gravy, spaghetti, macaroni and cheese – she taught me how to cook all of it," Kay said.

Billy supplemented whatever Kay cooked with his familiar blend of raw eggs, milk and ice cream. By the time he left Southeastern and joined the Cleveland Browns, he weighed 228 pounds.

Size was no longer an issue. Speed was. When Billy reported to training camp, he watched defensive linemen run 40 yards faster than he could.

However, when the linebackers lined up for a backpedaling drill, Billy outran all of them. That got his coaches' attention. So did his hand strength.

The Browns once found a scouting report that an opposing coach left in his Cleveland hotel room. His assessment of Billy was in large, bold type: "Don't let him get his hands on you."

Billy was lifting weights long before many football players were. He also was lifting bales of hay. And maybe, his homemade protein shake eventually was converted into muscles that would enable him to bring down any NFL ball carrier he could get his hands on.

His grip was enhanced by thick fingers that were used to milk cows when he was 15 years old.

"At one time, I had the largest ring size in the NFL," he said. "Size 18."

But ring size isn't an NFL "measurable." Neither was someone's backpedaling speed. Nor was there a number to indicate someone's hand strength.

Twelve rounds passed before Billy was drafted. But he wound up playing 11 seasons - mostly as a starter - in the NFL.

One of his highlight plays received national attention. He intercepted a Joe Namath pass and returned it for a game-clinching touchdown in the first "Monday Night Football" game.

But fans had no idea what went into that one play. They weren't privy to all the lifting, practicing and eating that eventually turned a 9-year-old's dream into reality, and proved so many people wrong along the way.

Billy couldn't even make third-team all-district as a high school junior. Most college recruiters wrote him off as too small.

But the same player who couldn't make third-team all-district as a junior made all-state as a senior. He began his college career as a sixth-string linebacker and was starting by the end of his freshman season. He was drafted in the 13th round by the Browns but soon became a fixture in their defense.

Long after his NFL career, Billy was still proving people wrong.

In 2008, he underwent successful heart-bypass surgery. At the time, Kay was concerned about what came next.

After heart surgery, patients are hooked up to a ventilator, which does their breathing for them. But once patients regain consciousness while on the ventilator, they feel as though they can't breathe, so they're apt to panic.

That's what worried Kay.

"I asked the nurse what would keep him from pulling the ventilator out once he woke up," Kay said.

"We have orderlies here," the nurse said. "He won't pull the ventilator out."

As soon as Billy regained consciousness, he tore the ventilator from his throat. And when the orderlies tried to restrain him, he threw them against the wall "like ragdolls."

Too bad, the ICU crew didn't have access to that old NFL scouting report: "Don't let him get his hands on you."

The Talking Cow

My newspaper career began at 15. And it began at the bottom.

I was assigned the most menial duties at a weekly newspaper, and I had the ink stains to prove my lowly status. The least pleasant of my chores was cleaning the small press that printed The Watchman, which was produced in Clinton but served all of East Feliciana Parish.

O.B. Chase, The Watchman's veteran linotype operator, was quick to notice that ink seemingly was drawn to me as though there were some chemical connection between us. No one else in the long line of teenage press cleaners ended the job with more ink stains than I did, O. B. said more than once.

That didn't bother me. Even then, I knew my future was as a writer, not a pressman. So, I bided my time cleaning the press, folding and wrapping papers, and absorbing as much of O.B.'s wisdom as I could.

The only advantage to folding and wrapping papers was the counting, which helped pass the time. I could count how many papers were folded before the machine broke down. I also timed myself wrapping papers that were mailed to subscribers outside the immediate area.

"Dr. No," a James Bond movie, provided the incentive for my personal folding record. Mike Felps and his sister, Becky, were picking me up at the paper on their way to Baton Rouge for the movie.

O.B. noted my speed and wondered why I couldn't always be that efficient. We both laughed, and I left for the movie.

Once, while wrapping papers, which were sent to readers all over the country and beyond, Roland Huson, who co-owned the paper with his wife, Malva, noticed that I had made more than three turns around a group of papers with the yarn.

"Only three," he said, as he kept on walking.

That made a lasting impression.

I remember reading a magazine article about husband-and-wife journalists who left the daily newspaper business to buy a weekly paper in rural America. The reality didn't match the fantasy.

Deadlines sometimes can be as unforgiving on a weekly newspaper as a daily one. And you must be capable of doing everything necessary to put out the paper.

The Husons were masterful at publishing a weekly newspaper, and their skills complemented one another. Miss Malva could write and was as good an editor as a 15-year-old aspiring journalist could hope for. Mr. Huson knew the business through and through.

Most importantly, he knew that if you wanted to make a living in the weekly newspaper business, you better be frugal. And you better notice when some absent-minded teenager is making a fourth turn with the yarn.

Both Mr. and Mrs. Huson were inducted into the LSU Journalism Hall of Fame, and I was honored to have written references for them, though they hardly needed anyone to vouch for their considerable accomplishments.

Having made it through my first summer of newspapering, I was looking forward to the fall. Although I was about to be published for the first time, I was overqualified for the job.

Since I also had learned to type that summer, I was already writing game stories in something comparable to Associated Press style. I would watch a baseball game on television and then type my account of it as fast as possible, as though my job depended on meeting an imaginary deadline.

My deadline with The Watchman wasn't nearly as pressing. Basically, I had until Tuesday to turn in my account of the previous Friday's Clinton Eagles football game.

I would call coach Hubert Polk for a quote about the next week's game. He called me, "Little Bud," a reference to then-Morning Advocate sports editor Bud Montet.

Bud and I did have something in common. Just as he wrote a complete play-by-play account of every LSU football game, I ignored no play of an Eagles game.

There was financial incentive for those lengthy game stories. I was paid 10 cents a column inch. So, a typical game story might be worth more than $3.

The editing was worth more than $3 a story, though. Miss Malva had a deft touch. She made corrections but was always encouraging. And if she ever became flustered sifting through my amateurish prose, she never showed it.

In the middle of the football season, commas became the subject of my 10th-grade English studies. My next story for The Watchman reflected that. I don't think I wrote a sentence without a comma. Even then, Miss Malva maintained her patience while citing the excessiveness of my punctuation.

I continued writing accounts of Eagle's football games for the next two years. The parents of players probably were grateful for the scrapbook material. I can't imagine anyone else reading the stories from opening kickoff to the final play.

But when you're being paid by the column inch, every play counts.

When I returned to The Watchman a few years later, almost everything had changed except O. B. He was still the glue.

The biggest change was the ownership. The Husons had sold the paper to David and Marilyn Goff. The next biggest change: my pay and title. I no longer was working by the column inch. I had a salary. And I no longer was merely a Clinton Eagles football correspondent. I was the editor of the paper.

I was only 20 years old.

"Looks like you and I are the only ones who came back, Deano (another nickname of mine)," O.B. said.

Twice, under different owners, O.B. quit The Watchman. Each time, after pleadings from the owners, he returned.

To their credit, they realized O.B.'s value. In fact, he was almost indispensable.

He showed up like clockwork, usually wearing jeans and a khaki shirt. If there had been a hall of fame for linotype operators, he would have been in it. He adeptly and swiftly struck the linotype keyboard while singing whatever popped into his head, usually "The Great Speckled Bird."

He never attended college but knew English grammar as well as any journalist and could spell better than anyone I ever met. He didn't downplay his abilities, either.

One day, a stranger walked through the production section of our building. Observing all the machines, she wondered if they eventually might take the place of the human work force.

O.B. never let observations like that pass without a comment.

"Machines make mistakes," he said. "I don't."

But if you made a mistake, he never forgot it. When I returned as editor, he reminded me of the time I was assigned to rearrange various fonts of type. I pulled out a narrow drawer too far, scattering the metal letters all over the floor.

As I was about to begin the challenging task of correcting my blunder, Mr. Huson waved me off. "You don't let a tornado return to the scene of the crime," he said.

O. B. could give a blow-by-blow account of that story, and I didn't mind listening – even though I was the punch line. I've never enjoyed working with anyone as much as I did O.B.

The original plan was for me to edit the paper for the summer between my junior and senior years. But I was having so much fun – and I was making money – that I passed up an opportunity to be sports editor of LSU's school paper, The Reveille, and continued as editor of The Watchman through my senior year, almost until the day I was inducted into the Army.

Working fulltime while commuting to LSU wasn't easy. But I never had more fun in the newspaper business.

Linotype operator O.B. Chase was a Watchman legend.

I wrote about everything from governmental meetings to Little League baseball games. However, my joy was writing opinionated columns. I wrote a general-interest column and a sports column almost every week. Sometimes, I even wrote an editorial, too.

Some of it was horrible. But at that stage of my career, I wasn't big on self-criticism. So, I wrote away with no regrets or supervision.

I'm sure if someone from "outside" had been hired to edit The Watchman and written some of the things I did, the local citizenry might have felt compelled to beat the hell out of him. But since I had grown up there, the consensus opinion of my columns was something like, "Oh, that's just John Dean trying to be funny."

That assessment wasn't far off. My philosophical stance on column writing at the time was something like: "When in doubt, make fun of it."

I made fun of everything.

I wrote that Clinton's post office was so inefficient we should consider reinstituting the Pony Express for delivery. My mother had a great sense of humor, but she still had trouble with that column.

"What are you writing this week?" she asked me as I was typing away on my portable typewriter at the dining room table.

"It's a column on the post office," I said.

"What are you saying about the post office?"

"I'm recommending that the Pony Express would be an improvement," I said, half-smiling but not looking up from my typewriter.

"John, those are my friends."

"It's just a column," I said. "They shouldn't take it personal."

Mother walked away without further comment, but I thought she understood. She was much smarter than I, had a way with words and could be very opinionated. She would have made a great columnist.

I was harder on the Police Jury, the parish's governing body, than I was the post office – mainly because the police jurors made my job more difficult. It wasn't just that I was writing an account of their meeting for The Watchman, I also was a correspondent for the Morning Advocate in Baton Rouge. The larger readership meant more pressure.

And getting things right wasn't that easy since the jurors often had three conversations going simultaneously. Some of those conversations had nothing to do with governing the parish. For example, in the middle of one meeting, a juror told a story about having what he thought was a dead bobcat in the back of his truck. But the bobcat suddenly returned to life while the juror was driving.

Surprisingly, I can't tell you how that story ended. Since I would have to write a story on the meeting for a daily paper that afternoon, I had to shift my attention to whether the jury had authorized paving a rural road.

This paragraph synopsized my editorial: "One person recognized by the chairman should be the only one talking. Everybody else doesn't have to be listening but they could keep quiet so that if there happened to be one person, like a reporter, trying to understand what was being said, he could do so."

Despite the condescending criticism from a 19-year-old, no one on the police jury seemed bothered by my editorial. They probably assumed "John Dean was just trying to be funny" and continued conducting meetings as they always had.

Fortunately, I had an inside source. Doodle Andrews, the board's secretary, was my interpreter. After a meeting, I would ask Miss Doodle what had just transpired and also what was most relevant from a news perspective.

I think she felt sorry for me, as she would have anyone who was trying to make sense of those meetings. She quickly gave me a concise report that I could put in readable fashion for anyone waiting for news on a paved road.

Regrettably, Miss Doodle's son, Billy Andrews, was the subject of one of my columns. The star of Clinton's 1962 state championship team, Billy was already a starting linebacker for the Cleveland Browns.

NFL commissioner Pete Rozelle recently had disciplined prominent players for their gambling. He also had demanded that star quarterback Joe Namath give up his interest in Bachelor's III, a popular New York bar and night club that was frequented by mobsters.

That gave me the idea for a sports column, which I wrote in the form of a letter to the NFL commissioner. I wrote that Andrews should be investigated over possible Mafia ties.

I gave a number of ridiculous reasons, one of which was his sister-in-law was a member of a parish gambling syndicate. She played canasta weekly.

The column was obviously satire. However, I included a photo of Billy and his older brother, Charles Henry, next to the column with a caption speculating that they might be figures in an investigation by Rozelle. Someone even asked Billy's wife, Kay, if Billy were in trouble.

But I got another column out of it. The following week, I wrote a column explaining satire. It was far more condescending than what I wrote about the police jury.

Satire also led to the greatest phone conversation of my career.

In my first summer as editor, the parish school board had a federal mandate to implement a desegregation plan. I decided to offer my assistance.

In what might have been my all-time worst column, I wrote that a cow named Dozier had wandered into The Watchman and outlined a school desegregation plan. I also wrote that Dozier was on LSD.

My original plan included shepherding a real cow into the newspaper building one night and taking a picture of it. I consulted with two of my former classmates, Man Williams and J. Ed. Hall, and asked if that were doable.

They liked the idea at first. But after further analysis, they concluded no cow on their property could be trusted to behave in a civil manner inside a newspaper office.

I was disappointed but determined to have accompanying "art" with my column. I found a photo of an award-winning 4-H cow, cut it out and enlarged it for publication. That became Dozier.

Unlike my column on Billy, there was no immediate backlash. Clearly, this was "just John Dean trying to be funny."

The backlash came later. A few weeks after the column had been published, I received a telephone call from an irate woman in Baton Rouge.

She was infuriated that I had accused her son's prize-winning cow of being on LSD.

My first reaction was stunned disbelief. Then, I laughed. A lot.

She didn't laugh. She said this was a serious matter.

So, I tried to reason with her, emphasizing that I also had quoted the cow. And everyone knows a cow can't talk, right?

By the time our conversation ended, she had settled down and seemed assured that the reputation of her son's cow had not been impugned.

I couldn't wait to recount the conversation with O.B., so he could comment on the intellect of our average reader.

My last column for The Watchman wasn't satire. It was about O.B. – more specifically, about how important he was to the paper and me.

I closed it with a saying he used often and applied to anyone within hearing distance.

"Carry on like you live," he said. "Slow and sloppy."

An 'Indian Outdoorsman'

Louisiana is called the Sportsmen's Paradise for a reason. The Great Outdoors isn't too far away no matter where you live.

For me, the Great Outdoors was my backyard, which extended from the backdoor steps to a back street, a full block off Plank Road. No registration was required, and my hunting season was random. All I had to do was pick up my BB gun and open my eyes to the feathery game at my doorstep.

The only restriction, set by my mother: I couldn't shoot mockingbirds, cardinals or redheaded woodpeckers. At the time, I didn't really understand why they were off-limits, but I was comfortable functioning within those boundaries.

My favorite target was a brown thrasher. Not only was it a sizable target, it moved slowly and usually at ground level. Blue jays also were easy targets. They were tougher, though. BBs bounced off their chests.

The field tilted in my favor when Santa Claus brought me a pellet gun for Christmas. Blue jays then became as helpless as the brown thrashers in the face of my arsenal.

I never hunted bigger game, such as ducks, quail, turkeys, or deer. My only other hunting experience was limited to squirrels in St. Helena Parish. I didn't hit anything.

Since I have become an avid birder in recent years, I feel guilty about murdering birds in my backyard. It's hard enough for a bird to survive migration. Four out of five don't. And there I was attacking birds that didn't stray any farther than my neighborhood. I even kept a running total, which reached 19 before I lost interest. What was wrong with me?

Maybe, there was a genetic component. My brother told me our grandfather, J. B. Dean, was a great shot – so good, in fact, that he made money off his marksmanship. His specialty was quails. He even shot a pair of rare albino quail, which he sold to a New Orleans restaurant. The restaurant owner then mounted them on a wall – for atmosphere, I guess.

Most of my friends ventured deeper into the woods in their animal pursuits. They shot whatever was in season, gigged frogs, and fished. I caught a few fish in ponds with a cane pole, but not enough to bother keeping a total or to keep me interested. I gave it up after hooking my friend, Bill Bennett, in the hand after a wayward backswing.

Maybe, I would have been better off without a pole but I was never introduced to fish-grabbing. It was as routine as riding a bike to some of my peers. They made it sound so simple.

They would find a hollow log in the early spring when the fish were nesting. Once the male and female hunkered down in the log to protect the eggs, they would grab away. It seemed as easy as shooting brown thrashers.

When the fish-grabbing process was described to me, I didn't feel as bad about shooting backyard birds. Fish-grabbing seemed much more sinister. It was a home invasion of sorts. And as much as I regret having killed birds, I never killed one in its nest.

In the Sportsman's Paradise, all that outdoor stuff went with the territory. And the participants ranged from the novice to Talmadge Bunch.

He was "Sheriff Talmadge Bunch" for 20 years. Although at no time in my childhood did I ever think, "Talmadge probably will end up being sheriff of East Feliciana Parish," it's not all that surprising. After all, it is an elected office. And you didn't need to take a poll or survey to know how well liked Talmadge was. So were his parents, George and Pauline.

Never mind that Mr. George's job as game warden didn't always lend itself to high approval ratings. As Mike Felps told me, "He could make you feel good about being arrested."

Talmadge was born the day after me on July 23, 1948. We grew up in the same town, but worlds apart. His world was opened to him by his father, the game warden. They often went into the woods together, but Talmadge wasn't afraid to venture out on his own.

He stayed with his grandmother when his mother and father were at work. But staying inside was a challenge for him. One day, an 8-year-old Talmadge couldn't resist the call of the wild. He packed some worms into his pockets and headed for a pond – not the one behind his house, but a mile away.

When his parents returned from work, Talmadge was nowhere to be found. Sheriff's deputies got involved.

"They even dragged the pond (behind his house), thinking I might have drowned," Talmadage said.

His mother was in tears when she saw him coming up the driveway. As traumatic as that might have been for his parents, they probably realized as Talmadge grew older, there was no safer place for him than the outdoors. It was as much a home to him as it was to all the critters that so fascinated him.

"Talmadge was one of these Indian- type outdoorsman," Charles Henry Andrews said. "He was the type that could do about anything."

But he did it like nobody else.

"He could sneak up on a turkey on a flat ground crawling," Mike said. "A turkey has better vision than anything I know of. One time, I was in a tree 150 yards away from a flock of turkeys at the end of the field. I leaned up maybe four inches for a shot, and they took off."

His point: animals functioned differently around Talmadge.

Mike told me about somebody wanting a raccoon. So, of course, they called Talmadge.

"Talmadge had him on a string," Mike said. "The coon kept wrestling until it came off the string. So, Talmadge put his foot on the side of the coon's head and tied him back up like nothing had happened.

"When coons are wild, they will bite the fire out of you. If that had been anybody but Talmadge, they would have gotten bit to hell and back. He's just had a sense."

His sense wasn't limited to turkeys or raccoons. It seemed to work with every animal he encountered. And he encountered plenty.

As a teenager, he would take a break from bush-hogging a field, jump off the tractor and chase rabbits. He caught what he chased, too – sometimes as many as seven or eight in a day.

"The weeds were about four or five inches high, and I think their feet would get tangled up in them," Talmadge said, as if to minimize his achievement, or at least give the rabbits an excuse for being caught by a human on foot. It was as though he could anticipate their movement, the way a cat does its prey.

"I would take them home to my uncle who would use them to train his hunting dogs," Talmadge said.

Talmadge also climbed trees and caught raccoons as easily as he ran down rabbits in fields. Sometimes, he had help – like when he went after flying squirrels.

His friend, Jerry Freeman, would climb a tree and roust the flying squirrels from their nest. Talmadge would wait below and off to the side, positioning himself where he thought they would land. Sure enough, he knew. They hit his chest and legs. And in some cases, became a pet.

He brought one home to his girlfriend, Sue Johnson, who later became his wife. That didn't go well.

"He got out of his cage, and bit Mr. J.J. (Sue's father)," Talmadge said. "He threw him in the commode and flushed him down the toilet."

Grabbing fish comes easy to Talmadge Bunch. But he also has caught everything from alligators to rabbits.

Although Talmadge lived most of his life in Clinton, he also attended Chamberlain Hunt Academy in Port Gibson, Miss. Right away, he capitalized on the new hunting grounds.

"I probably caught 35 chipmunks," Talmadge said. "I took them back to Daddy. I think I got chipmunks started all over Clinton."

Talmadge's ability to catch things spread through town. Need an alligator evicted from your yard? Call Talmadge. Lose a parrot to the wild? Call Talmadge.

Talmadge remembers an alligator crawling around town. "I don't how he got across highways, but he did," Talmadge said. "He must have done it at night."

Talmadge eventually got the gator via top-water plug. "They'll strike at anything," he said.

But he didn't always need tools to catch an alligator. He could do it with his hands, as though neither the challenge nor risk was any greater than if he were reaching for a chipmunk. He wasn't reckless about it, though.

Hand-grabbing alligators was limited to those 4-feet long or smaller. He caught them around the head and closed their mouths.

Sounds so easy, it's a wonder every man, woman and child in town wasn't an alligator hunter.

But everybody in town didn't have Talmadge's level of anxiety. On a scale of 1-10, 10 being the highest, Talmadge's anxiety level must have been a minus-2. If he reached into the water with intentions of grabbing a fish, he wasn't the least bit unnerved when he realized he had his hands on an alligator.

"I never had a fear of animals," he said.

Nothing that happened in Clinton's animal kingdom changed his mind. He was bitten by a non-poisonous snake once. Other than that, he was pretty much unscathed.

But fearlessness alone won't enable you to catch animals. Talmadge had that sixth sense about it – an ability to figure out what an animal would do next, or where it might go.

That's how he caught a stray parrot.

"I was still in high school when there was a parrot flying around town," Talmadge said. "He was running with a bunch of blackbirds. I found out where he was roosting in a cane thicket."

The rest was easy for Talmadge. He waited until darkness, then carefully sawed the cane on which the parrot was perched, about 40 to 50 feet off the ground. Unaware that the cane was moving, the parrot was soon within Talmadge's reach. Game over.

Talmadge also could put food on your table.

Then-sheriff Arch Doughty could cook almost anything on his backyard grill and make it taste good. Possum was one of his specialties. He had a cage where he could keep the possum before they were fit for cooking.

But to cook a possum, you have to catch a possum. That's where Talmadge came in. Often, after outwitting one of the creatures, he would call Mr. Arch to let him know: "I left a possum in the cage."

Almost any story about Talmadge seemed to involve an animal – or fish.

When he was baptized in the Amite River as an adult, the minister was astounded when Talmadge came up holding a minnow in his hand.

"He's the only person I ever baptized who caught a fish," the minister said.

Talmadge still goes fish-grabbing with his friends, Bill and Cliff Hurst. Sometimes, he's content to instruct the younger generation, including his son, Bennett, on the art.

"We'll sit in the boat and tell them how to do it," Talmadge said.

But even as he approached 70, he wasn't averse to swimming 10 to 12 feet deep in pursuit of a trapped fish. And there's a backyard full of rabbits as evidence he hasn't given up on catching animals. He raises them, too - much to his wife's dismay.

"My goodness, there are rabbits all over our yard," Sue said. "They've eaten up thousands of dollars worth of roses that I planted."

Even though Sue never shared Talmadge's infatuation with animals, her father assured her years ago there was an advantage to it.

"It will keep him out of the bars," Mr. J.J. said.

While Talmadge still hunts and fishes, he's out of the sheriff's business. He doesn't have any battle scars from that, either.

Strangely, the hunter/sheriff never carried a gun. He didn't believe he needed one. He even likened himself to "Andy of Mayberry."

I asked him if he ever had a gun pointed at him.

"Just once," Talmadge said. "It was a domestic dispute. Fellah came to the door with a shotgun. But we talked a bit, and then he went on to jail with me."

Find Another Place to Sit

Warren Record got a valuable education in school-bus riding on his very first trip. The lesson: There's more than one place to sit.

He was 6 years old and in the first grade. Or, as he described himself, "A snotty-nosed kid."

He took the first seat he saw, next to an older woman. He estimates Sandra Siebert was in the sixth grade at the time.

And she apparently wasn't attracted to snotty-nosed kids.

"She beat me up," Warren said.

And then?

"I found another place to sit," he said.

Warren's bus driver was Lanier Brashier, who was responsible for transporting many of the Ethel-area children to school. Warren said one of the Siebert children – not the one who beat him up – gave Brashier the nickname "Stymie."

Hopefully, it had nothing to do with the Scottish meaning of the word: "Blind man."

Mr. Brashier, whose vision apparently was just fine, smoked a cigar and kept a stick nearby.

"He carried the stick to get your attention," Warren said. "He said, 'sit down and shut up.' "

Gerald Ray Schober doesn't remember his first bus ride any more fondly than Warren does.

Like Warren, he was in the first grade when he boarded the bus for the first time. His mother, Edna, tried to reassure her first child by telling him how she also once rode the bus from her home on Plank Road into Clinton. In fact, her brother drove a school bus for a while.

That didn't make Gerald Ray any more at ease, though. But his mother probably was more upset than he was.

"She drove behind the bus the first few days," Gerald Ray said. "I remember looking out the back of the bus to see if she was still there. I think she was crying."

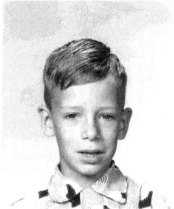

It helped that Gerald Ray had one family member on the bus. His cousin, Linda Denham, was older and comfortable riding the bus to school.

Gerald Ray eventually became comfortable, too. And many of the passengers became his extended family.

David Sobers became a "flag boy" when he was only 12.

David Sobers was one of his best friends. David was the first on the bus since his uncle, Arthur Sobers, was the driver. They lived next door to each other.

Because of his family connection, David assumed more responsibilities on the bus when he was 12. No longer was he just a mere passenger. He was the "flag boy."

Anytime a passenger had to walk back across the road after exiting the bus, David had to lead the way. His job was to make sure no one tried to pass the bus while the student was crossing the road. As a precautionary measure, he held up a pole with a red flag attached.

"It was just a piece of cloth attached to a pole," David said. "A homemade thing."

But it worked just fine. No motorist ever struck a child on David's watch.

Each bus apparently had its own protocol. But Mr. Arthur had only one rule: "Don't throw anything out the window."

On David's bus, the older you were, the further to the back you sat.

So, he started out on the front row as a first grader and ended up on the back row as a high school senior.

"You usually sat on the same seat for the entire school year," David said.

The starting point was Arthur's home on Hwy. 412. He then moved on to Plank Road and later made his way to Hwy. 958, where they picked up Glancy Schmidt, another great friend of Gerald Ray's.

Gerald Ray met Glancy at church. But his first acquaintance with those other friends came on the bus.

They started out on a smaller bus, which had about 20 seats. As the area grew, so did the bus. By the time, Gerald Ray was in high school, the standard-sized bus could carry as many as 40 passengers.

And by that time, "we were like a family," Gerald Ray said.

Stories about school buses got my attention, perhaps because I experienced them on such a limited basis. While I had to walk only a block to school, I rode the bus from our high school to the gymnasium for physical education class or basketball practice. The short trip didn't prevent me from speculating on the skills of our driver.

I was on board when one driver backed into a parked car. I coupled that with a more harrowing story and concluded that missing out on the complete bus experience wasn't all that bad.

Seventh-grader Selwyn Blouin hadn't been in Clinton long, after moving from Baton Rouge, when he witnessed a bus accident that could have been much worse.

He was seated by the window just behind Miss Ham when she slumped over at the steering wheel as the bus crossed Pretty Creek bridge. Selwyn doesn't remember what he did next but guesses, "I was probably hollering like hell.'

He does remember what Ann Hall did.

A tall, slender basketball player, Ann was seated across the aisle and one row back from Selwyn. When Miss Ham passed out, Ann sprang into action.

"She grabbed the wheel and started turning it," Selwyn said. "Because she was jerking the wheel, only the front wheel of the bus went over the bridge. If not for that, the bus would have gone into the creek."

Thanks to her, no one was injured, except Ann.

"I think she hurt her knee when she did that," Selwyn said. "I remember her wearing a knee brace for a while after that."

After the Pretty Creek incident, Willie Smiley started driving the bus, according to Selwyn, who learned that the Clinton bus system was much more accommodating than the one he had experienced in Baton Rouge.

"The buses in Baton Rouge would just take us to and from school," Selwyn said. "It was totally different in Clinton."

When Selwyn played in the school band, Mr. Smiley would pick him up at his house on Friday and take him to high school for the football game. It was akin to having your own limo service. There was no other passenger on the bus except Selwyn. Then, when the game was over, the bus driver would take Selwyn home.

That kind of service wasn't unusual.

Linda Warm, who lived on the Liberty Highway, rode Mr. Hardwick's bus to school. But by the time she reached the fourth grade, she had a bus route of her own in mind.

She asked Mr. Hardwick if he would drop her off in downtown Clinton so she could buy a "Sugar Daddy" candy at Mr. Feierabend's grocery store.

"I thought I was something, because I had made that decision myself," she said.

Mr. Hardwick went along with her plan and dropped her off at the grocery story whenever she asked. Linda would buy the candy, then walk to school.

"I don't think my parents ever knew I did that," she said.

Claude Rouchon remembered Mr. Hardwick's wife sometimes drove the bus. He also remembered that she was quite capable of maintaining discipline.

He was only in the fourth grade when a couple of more experienced riders, Bobby Cross and Robert Blackard, decided to liven up the ride between pick-ups.

"They took paper and taped it to the ceiling of the bus," Claude said. "Back then, you could smoke. So, they lit the paper with cigarette lighters."

When other students started shouting "fire," Bobby and Robert knocked down the paper, but they still got an earful from Mrs. Hardwick.

"She was a tiny woman, but she went back there and gave them the riot act," Claude said.

Janice Rice had an altogether different transportation experience going to and from school. She lived on Idlewild Road, about seven miles outside of Clinton. Her transportation was a station wagon, driven by Mr. Cooper.

"Nancy and Mary Spencer rode in the station wagon, too," Janice said. "So did the Joneses – Tom, B. Beth and Ann."

Mr. Cooper always smoked cigarettes but was thoughtful enough to keep the window down and hold his cigarette out the window. He also was patient. If you weren't on time when he arrived, he would park the station wagon and wait.

There also was a perk to riding to and from school in Mr. Cooper's station wagon. Every Friday afternoon, he would stop at the Spar service station and buy a Coke and candy bar for his passengers.

Gerald Ray pointed out there was a perk to riding his bus, too.

Doris Irwin, a young, attractive teacher, would pass Gerald Ray's bus every day when he was in high school. That became the highlight of the ride home.

"We would all try to get on the left side of the bus at the window when she came flying by," Gerald Ray said. "We would shout and wave. And she would wave back.

"Then, when we would see her at school, we wouldn't even speak to her. We were too embarrassed."

Those passing glimpses of Miss Irwin were short-lived. She didn't teach at Clinton long.

Girls developed their own routine while riding the bus in high school. Ruth Anderson, Cynthia Young and Johnette Peairs would write notes to truck drivers and milkmen.

"They would pull up behind us when we were stopped and we would stick the paper up to the window," Ruth said.

The bus that served students south of Clinton had one tradition that included both boys and girls. And it stood the test of time.

David doesn't remember how it started. He just remembered that it continued from the first grade on through his senior year. On the last day of school, students tore up whatever paper they had and scattered it about the bus.

David's Uncle Arthur had to clean up the mess, but he didn't seem to mind, according to David. Maybe, he had an appreciation for tradition.

I would have liked to have been a part of that tradition. I think I would have liked being a "flag boy," too. But I was just a bus-riding wannabe.

Several years after I graduated, I acknowledged my fascination for school buses in a column I wrote as editor of The Watchman. It was one of my many failed attempts at humor – a satirical assault on the "yellow monsters" that clogged up our roads and sometimes backed into parked cars.

The only good thing about my column was the letter it elicited from a school bus driver.

Charlotte Ligon began her letter to the editor with: "Enclosed is my $4.00 and a request for a year's subscription to the Watchman. (I've been reading my mother-in-law's second hand, but after that brilliant article on the school bus I felt I should have this personification of literary genius in my home firsthand)."

She was even more sarcastic than I was.

"My 'monster' is of the smaller green flowered variety," she wrote. "But we operate on the same principle. That principle being to maintain some semblance of sanity and at the same time transport children safely to and from school. And until you've tried it, don't knock it."

She was right, of course. But what struck me most about school-bus-related stories was how well the passengers remembered those daily routine rides many years later. Also, how much they all genuinely appreciated their drivers.

They thought about those drivers the way I did many of my teachers. Like the best teachers, the drivers went above and beyond. And they showed how much they cared about their passengers along the way.

From what their former passengers told me, the feeling was mutual.

The Star of Our Class

The Clinton of my childhood wasn't defined by the city limits. It also included the surrounding countryside.

And it was marked by people, rather than signs.

My Clinton stretched in one direction about eight miles to the F.S. Williams store, just past the Crossroads, and not quite to Ethel, which was even smaller than Clinton. My friend and classmate, Manship "Man" Williams grew up in that store. So did his younger brother, Ray.

Man and Ray were just carrying on a family tradition. Their grandparents started the store. Their parents kept it going.

As the family grew, so did the store. Initially, it was more of a grocery store. Then, it morphed into a grocery/general store. But it expanded to include hunting and fishing equipment under Man and Ray.

Outdoorsmen were drawn to Man, who could speak so authoritatively on their hobbies. Customers came from Baton Rouge and even farther away.

I didn't realize how popular Man and the store had become until I made another one of those long, sad trips home.

He was thrown from a horse and killed on his home ground, not far from the store, in December 2005. I drove 600 miles and arrived at his church in time to stand in a long line of people waiting to pay their respects to the family.

Thousands of people either went to the church that evening or attended the funeral the next morning. That surely constituted one of the largest such gatherings in East Feliciana Parish.

And when I managed to get past the grief of losing such a close friend, I was proud – proud of how popular and appreciated my childhood friend had become.

He was a good baseball player, but not nearly the best athlete in school. He made decent grades and graduated from Northwestern State University, where he played in the school band.

But as I drove back to Knoxville after the funeral, as I thought about the line of mourners outside the church, I realized that Man was the star of our class.

The baseball field adjacent to the American Legion Hall, just outside Clinton, was named after Man, who coached youth league teams for years. The store's continued success was another testament to him.

And so were my memories.

When I teared up, Man's face would come to mind. Then, I couldn't help but smile, because I always remembered Man smiling or laughing.

My greatest certainty in 12 years of Clinton schooling was that I could make Man laugh.

Almost no one liked giving speeches in school. But I made the best of them. And my approach never varied.

I would memorize the speech as best I could, then hope we would be called on in alphabetical order. If not, my hand would shoot up almost in the same instant that our teacher first solicited speakers.

Once I had finished rattling off my memorized material, I was free to enjoy what was left of the hour. I had a plan for listening, just as I did for speaking. Basically, my listening plan consisted of staring at selected speakers.

The highlight was always Man's speech. My stare might have gone unnoticed with other students, but I knew Man would look at me, probably sooner than later. And when he did, his face would turn red and his familiar smile would break out. Sometimes, he would go beyond a smile and start laughing.

If I wanted a laugh, Man was always my go-to guy.

Never mind the world's greatest orators. To this day, Man remains my favorite and most entertaining speaker. And he didn't have to articulate a word. He only had to match my stare with a smile, or preferably, a laugh.

Man and I once teamed up for a debate in civics class. We were pitted against two girls, who were better students and better prepared. The topic: "Swimming in a Public Pool" vs. "Swimming in a Creek."

The debate was just underway when one of our competitors pointed out that you could get bitten by a snake in a creek. I anticipated that possibility before the debate, and - since our preparation had been limited to a few moments during the previous recess – had no counter response.

But I didn't need one.

"I swim in creeks all the time and I've never been bitten by a snake," Man said without hesitation.

That alone might have fallen flat. But Man followed it up by turning red and laughing as he turned toward the class, which, of course, responded with laughter of its own.

End of debate. We had won by acclamation.

Afterward, I realized that snakes were a recurring theme in our friendship.

Once, while spending a Saturday at Man's house, we ran across a small garter snake. I might not have given it a second thought if Man hadn't sprung into action. Like a good chess player, he was thinking several moves ahead.

He found a spare pot in the kitchen and put the snake in it. Meanwhile, in another corner of the house, Ray was trying to sleep off a bad cold. Man placed the pot in Ray's line of sight and tilted it just enough so that the snake would be the first thing Ray saw when he woke up.

Although Ray was only 7 or 8 years old, he was old enough to know the difference between a harmless garter snake and something poisonous. However, when you are waking from a deep sleep, there's not enough time to distinguish one snake from another. He screamed.

Man laughed away.

There would be punishment, of course. His mother, Miss Alberta, surely looked appropriately horrified upon learning that one son had treated another son so terribly. But no matter how stern her expression when she rendered Man's sentence, I'm sure she laughed later.

Even as she approached her 95th birthday, she still had a wonderful sense of humor. As a kid, I picked up on that right away and felt comfortable bringing humor to what might be regarded as serious situations.

For example, when Man was young, he invariably ran a fever with any illness. If he had a high fever, he sometimes would complain about seeing snakes on his bedroom wall.

So, whenever Man was too sick to go to school, I would call him as soon as I got home. I ignored small talk and got right to the heart of the matter. "What do you see on the wall?" I would ask.

I don't remember his responses. But I do remember that we laughed about it later.

We shared sad times, too.

Man's father, M. Ney Williams, worked two jobs. Not only did he help manage the F.S. Williams store along with Miss Alberta, he also had a career in education.

He was still in his 20s in 1950 when he coached Clinton to its first state championship in football. He later became the Clinton High principal and then school superintendent.

I benefited from his job promotions.

In the summer of 1964, Mr. M. Ney headed for Athens, Ohio, for a national school superintendent's convention at Ohio University. He took Man and me along for the long ride, which was nothing but a vacation for us.

In anticipating the trip, I didn't think much about a university dormitory stay. I had something much bigger in mind. In fact, all I could think about as I boarded their cherry-red station wagon on a Saturday morning was major league baseball.

Cleveland was out of our way. But Mr. M. Ney didn't mind. He also was a baseball fan. And any baseball fan could have appreciated our destination. We were headed for Cleveland's Municipal Stadium, where the Indians and New York Yankees had scheduled a Sunday afternoon doubleheader.

The Indians were OK. They had Leon Wagner and Vic Davalillo in the outfield. But the Yankees were in the middle of another dynasty. Mickey Mantle was in center field, and Roger Maris was in right.

With that in mind, the trip didn't seem too long. Mr. M. Ney was a regular iron man. He drove all the way and all through the night from Clinton to Columbus, Ohio. We checked into a hotel to get a few hours sleep, then got up the next morning and drove to Cleveland.

Fatigue wasn't a concern, but the weather was. It was grey and cool. Cool became colder when we took our seats in the stadium, which was situated on Lake Erie. I concluded that a summer day in Cleveland wasn't much different from a winter day in Clinton.

We were five innings into the first game when a slight sprinkle became a full-blown rain. The doubleheader was rained out, and we headed for Ohio University. That still ranks as one of my greatest sports disappointments.

Another trip turned out much better for us. This time, the driver was C.A. Charlet, Chuck's father. Chuck Charlet and Phil Graham also were along for the trip. Our destination was the 1966 Cotton Bowl in Dallas, Texas, where LSU would play unbeaten Arkansas, which still had a shot at the national championship.

Early in the game, Arkansas quarterback Jon Brittenum took a hard hit and went down. He was an outstanding college quarterback and one of the biggest reasons the Razorbacks entered the Cotton Bowl on a 22-game winning streak. One Arkansas fan even wrote a song about him. "Quarterbackin' Man" was the title.

So you can imagine how silent the pro-Arkansas crowd got when he went down. Man responded quite differently.

I probably should have mentioned earlier how talented Man was with a musical instrument, which in this case, was a bugle. He often brought it to games, where he played "Charge" or imitated Woody Woodpecker's signature sound, although that had nothing to do with sports.

This time, Man had something else in mind. As the "Quarterbackin' Man" lay on the field, our Man played "Taps." Poor taste? Sure. But we had an excuse. We were high school seniors.

The Arkansas fans, who were all around us, turned and glared at Man, whose faced reddened from the physical exertion but not from embarrassment.

I would have expected nothing less.

Things worked out for the best. Brittenum went back to the huddle and played the rest of the game. LSU pulled off the upset and ended Arkansas' winning streak and chance for a national championship. And my opinion of Man rose even higher.

My only regret about Man: I never told him about my last high school speech.

I had to give the salutatory address at our high school graduation, and I wasn't looking forward to the opportunity. I saw it as a challenge with no reward.

Once finished, I wouldn't get to sit back and stare at other speakers, with anticipation building for Man's moment on stage. And I wasn't just speaking to my class. The auditorium would be full of adults.

Nonetheless, I didn't vary from my game plan. With Mother's help, which was considerable, I typed up a speech and memorized it word for word.

No matter what I was doing that Friday, I was going over the speech in my mind, right up until when I was introduced at our graduation ceremony. As I walked from my chair to the lectern, I was reciting the speech just one more time. And then, I went blank. Not a single word came to mind.

What happened next seemed almost mystical. I stood in front of the microphone, and the words came out just as I memorized them.

But there were those few terrifying seconds of nothingness. Considering how I had treated other speakers, I deserved every second.

And Man deserved the last laugh.

A Miami Love Story

When Neal Manship Williams returned home from the military after World War I, he wasn't optimistic. He was ill and didn't expect to live long.

But he was thinking more about his wife, Faye, than he was himself. He wanted to make sure she was taken care of, so he put the F.S. Williams store in her name. The "F.S." stood for his wife's maiden name, Faye Sale.

He was wrong about his life expectancy, though. He lived for many more years.

But he was right about a store that was built in 1930 and lasted for more than 80 years before it burned down in 2011. The store sold just about everything except alcohol and supported three generations of families.

The success of the F.S. Williams Store was as much about family as business, because from one generation to the next, it remained a family business.

My strongest connection to the family was through Man, whose grandfather built the store; his father, M. Ney; and his mother, Alberta.

Man and I grew up together. And Man grew up in the store. So did his father.

Alberta spent much of her life in that store. But how she got there is a story worth telling.

She grew up on a farm in Murphreesboro, N.C., which wasn't much bigger than Clinton. Her father, David Francis, grew corn and cotton, but his most lucrative crop was peanuts.

Alberta remembers the cotton best. As soon as she got home from school, she headed for the cotton field.

Her life was predictable through high school. But when she graduated, her father told her he couldn't pay for a college education. However, he had an alternative plan. Although he couldn't afford to send her to college, he could send her to Miami, where his sister, Ann, lived. And since her husband had just died, she lived alone.

Alberta's bus ticket cost $10. She wouldn't realize how good of an investment that was until later.

She had never traveled that far or been to a city as big as Miami, but she was game.

"I didn't know what to expect," she said. "I didn't know what Miami was like. I had never been to a bigger city than Norfolk, Va."

But she was excited, not scared. "I had confidence in my daddy," she said.

More than 70 years later, she could remember the trip in vivid detail.

She remembered how a bus driver looked out for a young woman traveling alone.

"When I got to Charlotte, it was very late," she said. "I was having to transfer to another bus and had to wait several hours."

The bus driver didn't like the idea of her having to wait. He had her switched from Trailways to Greyhound so she wouldn't have to stay at the Charlotte bus station for several hours.

Next stop: Miami.

Her aunt helped her get a job at Burdines Department Store. But a social event proved more impactful.

A Navy officer and his wife, Jim and Louise Claspil, were renting a room in her aunt's home. Like so many others after World War II, the Claspils were getting ready to leave the service in 1946.

"We will be going home soon," Louise told Alberta. "But we're going to have a big party Friday night."

"I've got a new dress that I bought for a concert," Alberta said. "I'd love to go to the dance."

The lieutenant told her he didn't know of any single guys but he would ask the chaplain. They came up with one possibility: M. Ney Williams, who went by the name of Marshall Williams in the Navy.

"The three of us picked up M. Ney, because he didn't have a car," Alberta said. "Jim had a Volkswagon, so it was crowded."

Marshall handed her a corsage when they met. Then, they crowded into the Volkswagon, and Alberta sat on her date's lap.

The dance was in the ballroom of a large hotel. They hadn't been there for long when Marshall made an impression.

"We went outside on the balcony to dance," she said. "The music was so good.

"But he was a horrible dancer. Step to the left, step to the right. Step up and step back. That was it. I put up with it, though."

She was far more advanced as a dancer. Her father taught her when she was a child. He would play a harmonica while she would dance.

In between dances, Alberta and M. Ney managed to find common ground. Both had grown up "in the country." Their rural background became the focus of the conversation.

"We talked about where we lived," Alberta said. "We had a good time."

But when the night ended, she had no expectations. In fact, she didn't expect to hear from him again.

He surprised her the next day with a phone call and asked if she would have lunch with him the following Sunday. They met at church and walked to a nearby restaurant.

They sat on a bench near the beach and got to know each other better. That led to another date and then another. They saw each other almost every day until the day he told her he was leaving the service. And leaving Miami.

He was going back home to the F.S. Williams Store.

"I'll be back," he said.

She wasn't so sure.

"I really didn't expect he was coming back to Florida," she said.

But even though he returned to Louisiana, they stayed in touch through correspondence. She soon realized he didn't write any better than he danced.

Alberta Williams took a circuitous route from a peanut farm in North Carolina to the F.S. Williams Store.

"The worst script I ever saw in my life," Alberta said. "I could hardly read it."

Finally, he called one summer day to say, "I'll be coming to Miami." This time, she didn't doubt him.

When M. Ney returned to Miami in November, things had changed. He had a car, so they didn't have to ride the bus as they had before.

She was sitting in the car when he proposed to her. He handed her a ring that he had purchased at a jewelry store on the way.

Before he asked, she had an idea what was coming. And she knew what her answer would be. So what if he was lacking as a dancer or writer. She would say, "yes."

"I did want to marry him," she said. "I think you just kind of know those things, don't you?"

They were married in 1947. Afterward, they might have made marital history by choosing Murphreesboro, N.C., as their honeymoon destination. Her parents had been unable to come to the wedding so the honeymoon was the first chance M. Ney had to meet her family.

I wonder what their parents thought about her circuitous route to marriage. They had sent her from a farm in North Carolina to the big city, and she had ended up in rural Louisiana.

She had a new job, too.

When M. Ney returned home, he expected to help his parents manage the store. About that time, he was offered a job to manage the athletic department at Clinton High School, which basically meant being the football coach. But first, he would have to return to school to earn another degree. The job would be waiting on him when he finished.

His career in education was about to begin. So was her career at the F.S. Williams store.

Alberta was prepared for her role. She had worked in retail in both cosmetics and the thread department at that Miami department store. She didn't have any problem selling groceries or whatever else was on the shelves behind the counter.

Her in-laws made it easier for her.

"We got along great," she said. "They both just took me in. I loved them."

She also loved the store.

M. Ney would join her when his school day ended. M. Ney's brother, Tinker, helped as well.

"Tinker had injured his hip and leg in a vehicle accident when he was in the service during the war," Alberta said. "The injuries never healed. So, it was hard for him to stand long on that hard, concrete floor in the store."

Alberta seemed so at home in the store, you would have thought she had grown up in it, just like her husband.

That's how things usually worked out at the F.S. Williams store. There was Neal Manship and Faye before there was M. Ney and Alberta. Later, there was Man and Linda.

Linda met Man in college, and they were married a few months after he graduated. Then, like his father before him, he had a decision to make.

Man was offered a job as coach and teacher at Ringgold (La.) High School. After returning from the interview, he and M. Ney weighed his options. Man decided to work in the store where he grew up.

That meant Linda also would be working in the store. She had no problem with that, because she already knew Man's parents.

"They made me feel at home right away," Linda said. "Miss Alberta is a saint."

The odds might have been against marriages and work meshing so neatly. But those odds couldn't have been any greater than a young woman going from Murphreesboro, N.C., to Ethel, La., via Miami.

"I would have never thought something like that could happen," Alberta said. "I guess it was the way God guided me."

Losing A Friend

I was eating breakfast in a Nashville hotel dining area last Thursday when I noticed a woman crying uncontrollably in the lobby.

Strangely, I didn't wonder whether she had lost her husband or a parent. My first thought: "She must have lost a lifelong friend."

A few minutes later, after I checked my messages, that would be me.

Mike and I started the first grade together. Joined the Methodist church together. Graduated from high school together. Started LSU together.

And we took a bus ride from Clinton to New Orleans for our Army physical together.

He got out. I got in.

Thursday morning, I recalled another ride – from Clinton to Baton Rouge for a cattle auction. Mr. Sonny, Mike's dad, was driving. Mike and I were in the cab of the truck. We couldn't have been older than 12.

That's when I first wondered if Mike had a photographic memory. He gave me a scene-by-scene account of a Jerry Lewis movie - as though the film were unfolding in front of him on the panel of the truck.

I should have been bored to tears. Instead, I was fascinated that he could recall such details.

But I don't remember Mike most for talking. I remember him for listening.

That's why he was such a good friend to so many people.

He listened. He cared.

And even in the throes of a terrible disease, he kept listening and caring.

In Mike's condition, most people would have been consumed by the daily battle. Not Mike. MS slowed and crippled him. It didn't change him.

When we talked for the last time Monday night, he was more interested in what was going on with me than what was going on with him. So, I did most of the talking, and he did most of the listening.

I would like to think he's listening now.

Mike, I should have told you this when we left for the cattle auction: "I don't like Jerry Lewis."

That's what I wrote when Mike Felps died. I emailed it to Mike's daughter, Courtney, and her husband read it at his funeral.

I was at home in Knoxville between two basketball tournaments when Mike was eulogized and buried. That same day, I had to go to the emergency room. The symptoms – vomiting and intense pain in the lower right quadrant of my back - weren't mysterious, so I had self-diagnosed the problem before I arrived. I knew what a kidney stone felt like.

In a way, it was almost a relief. The nausea and pain numbed me to the loss. When you have a kidney stone, it more than gets your attention. It shuts out almost everything else.

But even amid the discomfort, the memories of Mike would come back. The memories began in childhood and mounted through adulthood.

I remembered him as the biggest, strongest boy in our class. In fact, he was the biggest player on our state championship football team when he was in the eighth grade.

I also remembered him as my friend in the wheelchair. Still, his size and strength mattered. Since the disease rendered his legs useless, he needed his strong arms to move him from his recliner to a wheelchair, and from his wheelchair to a bed. Despite the disease, he continued to work in the business office of a local clinic until the week before he died.

And in some ways, he seemed stronger than ever. I thought about that after our last conversation. I thought about it again after several people said they were shocked by the news of Mike's death.

He suffered from a dreadful disease. He was in a wheelchair. Yet people didn't see him as ill or crippled. They saw the strength that we first experienced on the playground.

I didn't hear this from Mike or his parents. But I remember when we were teenagers someone told me that Mike's parents, Mr. Sonny and Miss Mildred, constantly reminded him at a young age not to be too rough with the other children, all of whom were smaller. That probably didn't help him as a football player.

I'm not sure Mike's game-day training table served him or selected teammates well, either. Every Friday before a game, they would go out to his house on lunch break. Miss Mildred never failed to serve up a feast.

"Fried chicken, potato salad, rice and gravy – those were the staples," Billy Yarbrough said. "We ate like pigs."

I remember the desserts. Whenever I had a seat at the Felps' table, there were a couple of pies and cake waiting on the counter. And Miss Mildred always encouraged seconds of everything.

Mike didn't have any trouble filling out his 6-foot-3 frame. His playing weight was about 245, which meant he was bigger than almost all of his opponents. And he understood the game well.

Maybe, he would have been a better player if he had been more aggressive, especially against those smaller players lined up across from him. But he was good enough as he was. He made all-district and he was selected to play in the Louisiana High School All-Star game.

Mike was at his best as an offensive tackle, but he was assigned to defense in the all-star game. The opposing quarterback was Terry Bradshaw, who – long before he won four Super Bowl rings with the Pittsburgh Steelers – was an incredible high school athlete. He could throw a javelin as well as a football and was as big as some of the linemen he faced in high school. And much faster.

After the game, I asked Mike about his brief encounter with Bradshaw.

Mike recalled breaking through blockers and having Bradshaw in his sights. "I was just about to tackle him, and then he was 'over there,' " Mike said.

Mike then jerked his head to the side, reinforcing the impression that Bradshaw had escaped him so suddenly that he might as well have been beamed to the far side of the field.

Mike's evaluation of Bradshaw wasn't surprising. He was always good at recognizing someone else's strengths. I first noticed that when we were teenagers. And that unusual quality became more apparent in adulthood.

He often would tell me how impressed he was with someone's intellect. He would go on and on about how smart a friend or an acquaintance was. As I listened, I usually would think, "I bet they aren't any smarter than Mike." He was one of the smartest people I ever met. But he never thought of himself that way.

He was detail oriented and, as I already mentioned, a great listener. The combination made him an effective problem solver. He also had good ideas.

I told him once he would have made a good writer. He just laughed, as though the suggestion was ridiculous.

We were friends from the first grade on. The family connection went back further. My father was Mr. Sonny's sponsor in the Masons, which Mike later joined. I always appreciated how highly Mr. Sonny spoke of my father. Since my dad died when I was so young, my memories of him are based on what others told me.

Mike Felps was a once-in-a-lifetime friend.

My connection with Mike and his family strengthened when I got my driver's license. Then, I could drive a few miles out the Liberty Highway to their house whenever our family car was available.

Mike and I played basketball and badminton in the yard. We even had an indoor basketball court in his house. We converted a piece of metal and handkerchief into a makeshift basketball goal that was affixed above an open door. A tennis ball served as a basketball.

Mike would position himself closer to the goal and I would shoot from the perimeter. Our imaginary opponent got points with each miss.

I realize that doesn't sound like much. But we really enjoyed it. And after his death, when so many memories surfaced, I thought about something else. Mike always wanted me to shoot more. When I was "in a zone," and the tennis ball kept ruffling the handkerchief as it fell through the metal hoop, Mike became more excited about my run of success than I did.

We also played together one season on a Babe Ruth League baseball team. I can write with great certainty that I was never in a zone on a baseball field. Nor did I give Mike anything to get excited about. In fact, I contributed to one of his worst baseball memories.

Our team was playing in Woodville, Miss. Since the game was outside our league and wouldn't count in the standings, coach James McDowell decided to play his reserves for the first few innings. Woodville's coach wasn't as benevolent.

The worst part wasn't the game, but the infield practice beforehand. The infield was rock-hard clay, which seemingly had a few pebbles mixed in with the soil. To make matters worse, I was positioned at third – why, I'm not sure. But since the game didn't count in the standing, so what?

I was much more comfortable at second base, where my weak arm wasn't such a liability on throws to first. On that afternoon, the distance from third to first base, seemed farther than ever, as though Woodville had purposefully stretched the infield to exploit my weaknesses. I wondered, "Is Coach McDowell punishing me for something?

"And was he punishing Mike, too?"

Mike was the backup first baseman, making his first start. So, for that torturous round of infield practice that I thought would never end, he was on the receiving end of some of the worst throws you could have imagined.

He wasn't a slick fielder on his best day. And even slickness was no match for my throws. If I managed to cleanly field groundballs off the treacherous surface, the worst part was still to come. Since I strained to make the long, unfamiliar throw from third to first, Mike would have been better off catching knuckleballs with an under-sized mitt.

The ball sailed to his right, left and often came up short, forcing him to try and catch – or just block - short-hops on unforgiving ground. Once, determined not to come up short, I overcompensated and managed to throw the ball above and beyond Mike's reach.

I don't even remember the game.

Mike and I had more fun watching or listening to games. I'm not sure how or why, but Mike adopted the same teams as a teenager that I had acquired when I was 9 years old. Maybe, he was swayed by how much emotion I invested in the success or failure of the Pittsburgh Pirates and Baltimore Colts.

Sometimes, in the summer, when the Pirates were playing on the West Coast, Mike would join me in the living room, where our console radio could pick up the late-night broadcasts on KDKA in Pittsburgh.

As successful as the Colts were for the most part, they often came up short when matched against the Green Bay Packers' dynasty. That was fine with Mike's older brother, Sid. I'm not sure if he really was a Packers fan or just reveled in our suffering when the two teams played.

I remember watching an early-season Colts-Packers game in the mid-1960s at Mike's house. Mike and I sat on the sofa while Sid stretched out on the floor in front of us with his head resting on a pillow.

Mike and I agonized over almost every play. Sid never said a word.

Midway through the fourth quarter, a Packers defensive back intercepted a Johnny Unitas pass and returned it for a game-clinching touchdown. As Mike and I screamed at the turn of events, Sid still didn't utter a word. He just raised his head from a pillow, turned toward us and smirked.

Years later, Mike and I agreed it was the greatest taunt ever. And it was executed in silence.

Talk came easy between Mike and me except when we took that early-morning bus ride from the draft board office in Clinton to New Orleans for our Army physical.

We both drew low numbers in the draft lottery, so only a failed physical would keep us out. Mike had high blood pressure. I had a folder's worth of medical history that I had deluded myself into believing would keep me out of the Army – and, more importantly – Vietnam.

 After going through a series of examinations, I was the last person to meet with a physician. About seven or eight minutes into my medical monologue, I sensed he wasn't being moved by my knee or foot issues, all accompanied with documentation. He sat stone-faced as I kept yakking away, raising the volume as I felt a sinking feeling in my stomach.

"I see no reason you can't serve," he said.

And that was it.

Mike got a different verdict. His blood pressure was too high. He was a free man.

He didn't act like it on the return trip to Clinton. He wasn't going to celebrate while his friend sat in silence. He had too much empathy for that.

A few days after Mike's death, I called Billy Yarbrough to thank him for all he did for Mike during Mike's prolonged illness.

"You get a friend like Mike once in a lifetime," Billy said.

I felt the same way.

'Almost Ain't Good Enough'

My firsthand experience with cattle was limited to helping Mr. Mitchell "Big Mitch" McConnell vaccinate his hobby herd. But I realized at a young age that cattle served a more useful purpose.

They were important to the area's economy.

And much of that business centered around dairy cows. As beef cattle became less and less profitable, more and more people went into the dairy business. It was a logical progression since so many people had to put their land to use. John Allen Phares said his father, Mr. John T., told him in the 1950s there were 115 dairies in the area.

I associated the dairy business with tennis as much as with milk.

I learned the sport on Mr. Don Phares' court on the Liberty Highway, where I often partnered with Bobby McConnell or Greg Phares, Mr. Don's son.

Mr. Don, like his brother, Mr. John T., was in the diary business. So was Mr. Don's good friend, Frank L. Norwood, of Norwood.

Mr. Frank L.'s business went well enough that he had a hard-surface tennis court built at his home. I spent some of my most enjoyable Sundays when Greg and I were matched against Mr. Don and Mr. Frank L.

Although Greg was an outstanding player, I was average at best. And that wasn't good enough against the more experienced doubles team.

Neither age nor a bad knee impeded Mr. Don, who masterfully directed his shots to every corner of the court while loudly questioning the skills of his opponents at the same time. Mr. Frank L. posed a different problem in that he was a left-hander with a devastating curve.

The curveball came naturally to Mr. Frank L., who advanced as far as Triple-A as a pitcher in the New York Giants franchise when he was only 18. There wasn't much money in baseball at the time, and Frank L. became so homesick that he left the sport and returned to Norwood and his girlfriend. He and Miss Faye were married shortly thereafter.

"I used to tell Daddy that he kept me from knowing Mickey Mantle and Yogi Berra," his oldest daughter, Chrystal, said with a laugh.

Greg, who was a good baseball player himself, once coaxed Mr. Frank L. into pitching to him. Mr. Frank L. was in his 40s at the time and didn't even take time to warm up.

Greg, who had caught pro pitchers before, said he could barely handle Mr. Frank L.'s pitches because the ball moved so much.

Mr. Frank L.'s athleticism also came through on the tennis courts. Like Mr. Don, he had the ability to hit shots and take potshots at the same time.

Meanwhile, Miss Faye provided another distraction to whomever the Phares-Norwood team was competing against. She had a great laugh – almost a cackle, in fact – that invariably followed one of my errant shots.

Win or lose, I remember most of those Sundays as one big laugh-fest. The match often was followed by the sampling of a dairy product – homemade ice cream – and more laughter.

Even under more serious circumstances, Mr. Frank L. could make me laugh.

When I was editor of The Watchman while in college, one of my assignments was the East Feliciana Parish School Board meetings, which generally involved coming up with a desegregation plan in the summer of 1969.

Once, when Mr. Don was passionately expressing his opinion to the rest of the board, Mr. Frank L. turned his head slightly my way, smiled and winked. It was all I could do not to burst out laughing.

Laughter aside, I learned that the dairy business wasn't fun and games. I knew that Mr. Frank L. milked twice daily. A job that demands your presence at 3 a.m. is about as serious as it gets.

Clyde Chaney was another dairyman with a sense of humor. He also had a record for success as a high school basketball player; in the military, where he quickly ascended to the rank of chief warrant officer; and as a salesman in civilian life.

His oldest son, Ted, believed his dad was qualified to do just about anything – except run a dairy. But that eventually became Mr. Clyde's line of work, much to Ted's chagrin.

Ruth Chaney, Mr. Clyde's wife, was even less enthusiastic about the new venture. She had developed her opinion through experience. A native of Burlington, Vermont, Miss Ruth grew up in the business. Both her father and grandfather ran dairy farms.

She met her future husband in England, where they were stationed in the military. A registered nurse, Miss Ruth had no idea she was joining a family of future dairymen.

"She was totally against him starting a dairy," Ted said. "And she was against me being involved."

Ted wasn't keen on it, either. Although years later he would end up running the dairy, his involvement as a teenager often was limited to second-guessing what his father and his younger brother, Tom, were doing.

"They called me, 'The Showman,' " Ted said. "They said I just wanted to put on a show about having a farm. They didn't want me around unless they just had to have me."

Ted remembers several incidents in which he thrived as a critic.

"They were giving the cows shots of Terramycin, and the needle wasn't long enough," Ted said. "It would leave a big knot on those cows, and they would buck and carry on. I would say, 'You're not doing it right.' "

He also questioned Tom's tractor-driving judgment.

"Tom was coming back from the pasture, and he decided the pond was so shallow he could drive through it," Ted said. "I think he was about 14."

Apparently, that wasn't old enough to accurately ascertain the depth of the pond. The tractor was halfway under water when he realized he had miscalculated.

"I almost made it," Tom proclaimed.

" 'Almost' ain't good enough," was Ted's response.

Nor was Ted in agreement on how to handle a problem cow that wouldn't wait for the appropriate time to start grazing. Instead, she would crawl under the fence in pursuit of grass.

Ted said Mr. Clyde's strategy for the rogue cow was to shoot it with scatter shot. Unfortunately, Tom once tried to execute the same game plan. He got too close before opening fire and bloodied the cow.

"What are you accomplishing?" said Ted, ever ready with an instant critique. "The cow ain't gonna stop crawling under the fence."

The cow that kept crawling under the fence was named "Miss Edie," in honor of Ted's younger sister. It's only fair to point out that Mr. Clyde didn't know when he named the cow that it would misbehave on a regular basis.

No matter how much Ted enjoyed second-guessing, he couldn't argue that his father knew his cows. Mr. Clyde could call every one of his 50 cows by name.

While other dairymen had their cows tagged, Mr. Clyde didn't want to pay for the tag. His counter-move was to name each cow, usually after the name of the person that sold him the animal.

For example, a cow he purchased from McWillie Chambers became Opal, after Mr. McWillie's wife.

Distinguishing cows was important from an accounting perspective since their value was depreciated each year by age.

The IRS initially balked at Mr. Clyde's naming system, according to Ted. But Mr. Clyde's accountant, Oscar Webb, eventually convinced IRS agents that Mr. Clyde could tell Opal from Miss Edie and every other member of his herd.

Clinton's Billy Andrews might not have known his cows by name, but he learned the business well enough that he succeeded in the dairy business after his 11-year NFL career ended.

Neither he nor his family took to dairying right away, though.

Billy was 15 when he overheard his father, Mr. Charles Rist, telling his mother, Miss Doodle, that like so many other East Feliciana Parish land owners, he was about to enter the dairy business.

"The cow prices have fallen from 13 cents a pound to eight cents a pound," he told his wife. "We can't pay our bills at 13 cents.

"What are we going to do?"

Mr. Charles Rist already had the answer. He was quitting the beef cattle business for dairy farming.'

The transition wasn't smooth.

Billy and Charles Henry grew up dealing with beef cattle. Handling the cattle and lifting large bales of hay had built up their strength. Charles Henry, like his younger brother, also excelled in both high school and college football.

But that didn't make them an overnight success story as dairymen.

"Me and Henry would go down there to milk," Billy said. "We didn't know anything. All we knew was beef cattle. We were rough and tough with them."

Managing dairy cows required more finesse, as they soon learned.

On one of their first tries at milking, the cows tore away from the stanchions, support frames that were devised to hold the cows in place while they were being milked. Then, when the cows tried to escape, the stanchions became hung up on the door.

"We learned," Billy said.

Charles Henry, like Billy, became a successful dairyman.

The Rouchon family also was in the dairy business. The Rouchons moved to Clinton in the spring of 1957 after buying Holly Grove plantation. At one point, they were milking as many as 150 cows.

"Everybody thought we had money," said Claude Rouchon, who was one of my classmates, "because we bought a plantation. We were land-rich and cattle-rich, and had machinery. But we didn't have a lot of money.

"We built our own dairy farm. We were the first (in the parish) to have an automated system."

One morning, the Rouchon and Chaney dairy businesses became intertwined through a bizarre series of events.

Claude dated Dede Jones, who lived on Bank Street in Clinton. As he prepared to leave her house one evening, their conversation continued as he opened his car door, which was parked out front.

Suddenly, Claude was distracted by the smell of alcohol. Then, he heard a loud snore. He didn't have to look beyond his backseat for the source. A drunk had climbed into Claude's car before passing out.

Claude went back inside and called the sheriff's office. Deputy Albert Moffit arrived shortly and took the drunk to jail.

Problem solved, Claude assumed. At least, it was solved until Claude arrived at Clinton High the next morning and was confronted by an angry Tom Chaney.

Turns out, the drunk in the back seat of Claude's car was employed by Mr. Clyde. And his job was to milk cows that morning.

But as any experienced dairyman will tell you, you can't milk cows from a jail cell. Deprived of his No. 1 hand, Mr. Clyde had to rely on a backup, Tom.

"Tom was furious," Claude said. "He was adamant, pointing his finger at me."

"Because you put him in jail, I had to go milk," Tom said.

Just one more hazard of the dairy business.

No Guns or Cars

Juanita Morgan was crossing the street behind our back lot on the way to her father's store downtown. She didn't see the car until it was close enough to scare the driver.

The driver was as startled as Juanita was, but stopped just in time. Moments later, Juanita had made it to her father's downtown business, Zip's Auto Supply Store, which was next door to the original McKnight's Department Store.

By then, the driver already had called Juanita's mother, Jennie, to tell her what had happened. The driver was concerned. And with that call, she reinforced a feeling that Juanita and so many of us had.

"I always felt that everybody in Clinton was looking out for us," Juanita said. "Whatever success I attained, a major part of it was growing up in Clinton."

At a young age, her success seemed inevitable. She was smart, pretty, an outstanding swimmer, and was already excelling as a baton twirler when she was 8 years old.

If you had been told that the child would grow into a high school cheerleader or graduate with honors, as she did, you wouldn't have been surprised. That seemed like a natural course.

But despite her obvious potential, the course was anything but a straight shot. And along the way, we would realize that Juanita had something else going for her.

Even at a young age, she had a strong Christian faith and a determination to overcome a handicap that surfaced almost as soon as her potential did.

She was 9 years old when her handicap was spelled out in numbers. Her vision was 20-50 the school eye exam revealed.

Juanita heard a gasp from our fourth-grade class when those numbers were called out. They stood out amid all the "20-20s." Her teacher, Bernadotte Phares, immediately called her parents about the results of the eye exam.

Until then, there was scant evidence of a problem.

"When she was watching television, she would sit on the floor, then scoot up close to the set," her older sister, Vedera, said. "Daddy would tell her to move back.

"We didn't realize there was a problem. We just thought it was a habit."

After the eye test revealed something was wrong, Juanita's father took her to doctors in Baton Rouge first and then New Orleans. At first, doctors tested her for a possible brain tumor. Fortunately, that proved false.

Additional tests showed that she had a hereditary degeneration of the optic nerve. One of her cousins had the same defect.

I didn't understand the significance of that until years later. I doubt the rest of my classmates did, either. We just assumed Juanita had bad vision that would necessitate her wearing thick glasses.

In fact, she had a rare and serious eye disease that glasses couldn't correct. Her vision would only get worse as she got older.

"She was so pretty and composed," said Janice Rice Halphen, a childhood friend and classmate of Juanita's. "She had so much drama in her life, but she never let it show. Even at our 50th reunion, some people still didn't know how bad Juanita's vision was."

Ruth Anderson Dart began to understand the severity of Juanita's handicap when they were cheerleading together as high school seniors. As they prepared to lead the team through the goal posts onto the field, Ruth or another cheerleader would grab Juanita's hand before they made their entrance.

"She could hear the players coming, but they were just a blur," Ruth said. "We looked out for her."

Juanita's vision continued to deteriorate after she graduated from high school.

"I wish I had 20-50 now," Juanita said with a laugh 60 years after that classroom eye exam. "It's about 20-450."

But she never let those numbers define her. Neither as a child nor as an adult. Instead, she became defined by her response to the disease.

"She was one of the smartest and maybe the most disciplined student ever to go to school at Clinton," said Ted Chaney, who was a close friend of Juanita's older brother, Delos Morgan Jr.

Most of us didn't comprehend how disciplined. We just knew that she had to be near the blackboard to read what had been written. But she also had to study longer than anyone else to gain the same comprehension.

When Juanita entered Katherine Piker's high school math class, Miss Piker asked her if she took after her sister, Vedera, or her brother, Delos. Vedera was an outstanding student; Delos wasn't as interested in making good grades.

Miss Piker quickly figured out that Juanita was more like Vedera than Delos. She also figured out that Juanita would have to work harder to make high grades, because of her vision problem.

Ginger Pullig's friendship with Juanita began in the second grade. But she didn't fully appreciate her friend's resolve until they were college roommates at LSU.

"I would go to bed at a reasonable hour," Ginger said. "And Juanita would be up reading with a light and a magnifying glass. She would just study harder than all of us."

Juanita understood at an early age what was required for her to succeed. At the same time, she learned that the odds were against her achieving academic success.

"I overhead Dr. Clovis (Toler) talking to Daddy about my vision," Juanita said. "He said that I wouldn't be able to go to college, that maybe I could get a good husband who would take care of me. He said that out of concern for me."

Juanita didn't hear that and think "I'll show you." But she didn't give up on college, either. Instead, she took on the challenge daily.

"She called me from LSU one time crying," said Vedera, who is a retired school teacher. "She said she had failed a test, but that she knew the material. 'I don't know what happened,' she said.'"

Juanita's vision problems had been exacerbated by the fluorescent lighting and the nature of the test, which required her to color the multiple-choice answers into a box. She missed the boxes.

Vedera said Juanita was then allowed to take tests in a room with different lightning. Juanita also got an assist from Clinton's Rupert Thompson, who worked for the State of Louisiana.

"When she was at LSU, he got her a 'reader,' " Vedera said. "It was some kind of a machine that when you put a book under, it would magnify the words on a screen."

For the most part, Juanita received little help. Nonetheless, she succeeded at LSU, just as she did in Clinton.

She took on her challenges with a smile, not grim determination.

One of my favorite movies is "The Manchurian Candidate," in which Lawrence Harvey plays Raymond Shaw, who is captured and "brainwashed" by North Koreans as part of an elaborate plot to assassinate the President of the United States. His fellow soldiers, who also were captured, are programmed to believe that Shaw is a war hero.

Once they return home, whenever Shaw's name comes up, they say, "Raymond Shaw is the kindest, warmest, bravest, most wonderful human being I've ever known in my life."

That came to mind after talking to numerous former classmates. Anytime Juanita's name was mentioned, their responses were strikingly similar. But unlike in "The Manchurian Candidate,' the responses were heartfelt, not programmed.

Juanita still inspires everyone around her.

"I can't ever remember seeing her with anything but a smile on her face," was one.

"She was just a delight," was another.

And: "It was as though she never had a bad day."

As hard as Juanita fought to overcome her handicap, the fight didn't cost her a sense of humor.

When she had an early class one semester at LSU, she dressed in the dark, rather than turn on the light and risk waking Ginger. Our friend, Mike Felps, was in her class.

As she sat down next to Mike, he asked, "Little Juan (which is what Mike and I started calling her in high school), is that a new style – one red stocking sock and another yellow one?"

She just laughed about it.

In high school, some of her older school friends sometimes referred to her as "Helen" as in "Helen Keller." As cruel as that might sound, Juanita laughed about that, too. One of her teachers even referred to her as "Helen" once.

"I didn't take that in a bad way," Juanita said. "I guess I always tried to look for the best in people."

However, she did have bad days. One of the worst was when she reached her 15th birthday. Finally, she was old enough to drive.

"It was a big deal turning 15," she said. "But a doctor told me I would not be able to drive."

Her reaction: "I can see better than they think I can."

Aware of Juanita's determination to drive, Vedera reasoned with her.

"If I die, well no big deal," Juanita told Vedera, as a teenager might.

"But what if you hurt innocent people?" was Vedera's comeback.

That got Juanita's attention.

Nonetheless, her father asked Clinton High's driving instructor, Huey Tynes, to work with Juanita outside school.

"Thank goodness, Mr. Tynes had brakes on his side," said Juanita, aware that driving wasn't a good idea.

When Juanita saw Mr. Tynes again at our 20-year class reunion, she asked him: "Have you taught any blind people to drive lately?"

While she was at LSU, a friend wanted to teach her to use a handgun. He pointed to a tree in the distance as a marker.

"What tree?" Juanita asked.

That was the end of the shooting seminar.

"I don't handle cars or guns," Juanita said.

But she has handled everything else life has thrown at her.

When I interviewed Juanita, she was in the middle of a crisis, though you never would have detected it in the tone of her voice. She had been diagnosed with an aggressive form of breast cancer, which hadn't responded to chemotherapy.

Doctors were forced to revise their plan of treatment. They decided to remove the cancer surgically, then follow that up with radiation.

As if that weren't difficult enough, one medication had cost Juanita part of the feeling in her toes and fingers. Because of her blindness, that loss of feeling was crucial.

Her predicament seemed overwhelming. But when we talked on the phone and exchanged emails, she seemed more concerned about how I was dealing with the death of my friend, Mike Felps, than her own discomfort and uncertainty.

Since I had expressed concern for her health in my first email, she addressed it – but only at the end of her message. "A sidebar," she called it.

She graduated with honors from high school and graduated from college against all odds. She has had a wonderful marriage with her husband, Wayne Rizzutto; reared four children; been a longtime Sunday School teacher; and battled near blindness since childhood.

"It has left me pondering much – our priorities, etc.," she wrote of the cancer. "I see it as something that is allowing me to take account, evaluate, and appreciate – like old friends." Her quest received an unexpected boost in the mail.

For many years, Juanita has received books on tape from the State Library. She favored books on religion and Christian faith.

In the middle of her crisis, another audio book arrived. The title: "Thirty Days To Live."

"Can you believe that?" she wrote me. "The rest of the title was 'to live a risk-free life. The book is by a Christian author and is totally uplifting – with wisdom-filled suggestions based on biblical principles. It's about what changes would we make if we thought we only had 30 days to live."

But even before Juanita listened to the book, the emails she sent me were uplifting and full of wisdom. She could have written her own book.

As concerned as I was about her health, I never felt discouraged after any communication we had. Quite the opposite, in fact. I thought back to the Little Juan I knew in school and regretted that I hadn't known her better when we went to school together.

Even if I had, I wouldn't have understood how remarkable she was. You can't comprehend that as a teenager.

But now, with a lifetime's worth of perspective, I find her view of life – unimpeded by a faulty optic nerve - clear and inspirational.

War Heroes

The clues were more apparent in hindsight. They showed us where we were headed.

But within the secure confines of Clinton, La., those clues seemed dull and far away, even though one was only a short drive from downtown.

Harry Ebert built a bomb shelter next to his house on the Greensburg Highway. It was mainly a conversation piece, but it also was visual evidence of the Cold War that engulfed our generation.

It was the USA vs. Russia. Or, as we were taught in American History, Americanism vs. Communism, a six-week course that tested everyone's threshold for boredom. President Kennedy's television address on the Cuban Missile Crisis in the fall of 1962 was more compelling.

But the course and the crisis, like Mr. Ebert's bomb shelter, were all reminders that the Cold War could heat up at any time.

And when it finally did, it led us to Southeast Asia.

I was listening to the broadcast of an LSU basketball game when my number came up in the draft lottery. No. 153. Low enough to put me in harm's way.

My induction date was Oct. 8, 1970. While the outcome seemed inevitable, it was my nature to seek other alternatives – even when the alternatives reeked of desperation.

In desperation, I turned to Betty Hurst. She was the secretary for our local draft board. But she was more than that to me. She was my only recourse. And she was willing to listen.

After she explained my options for an appeal, I came up with a plan. Never mind that I had no grounds for an appeal. I would appeal anyway.

Miss Betty could have told me how ridiculous that was. But she didn't. Instead, she endorsed my strategy.

Although I couldn't win the appeal, I could delay my induction by going through the process. I wasn't dragged into the Army until Feb. 8, 1971, three months past my original induction date.

How much difference did that make? I don't know, but it couldn't have worked out any better. I spent most of my time in the Army as editor of the Fort Riley Post in Fort Riley, Kan., home of the famous Big Red One infantry division.

That greatly amused my friend, Mike Felps, who was a student of military history. He loved my Army stories, most of which consisted of my trying to avoid something through every devious means possible. But most of all, he loved the irony that someone as ill equipped for soldiering as I became a part of such a storied division.

The closest I came to combat was exchanging BB-gun fire with another platoon in basic training at Ft. Polk, and playing war games in Germany while the Big Red One fulfilled its NATO commitment to Europe. I suffered injuries during both ventures.

As I reloaded my BB gun in our fake fight, the spring slipped and sliced through my right forefinger, which was poorly positioned for the task. The irony didn't escape me. I had injured myself with a weapon that I had mastered in childhood.

I had no choice but to seek help from Drill Sergeant Aaron, who developed a loathing for me after my first few hours under his command. He just stared at me when I complained that I shouldn't be expected to perform KP (kitchen police) duty just a few hours after I had arrived at Fort Polk (La.) and spent the rest of the training cycle punishing me for it.

He stared again when I stood at attention and asked, "Where's the first aid station, Drill Sergeant?" I held up my bleeding forefinger to accentuate the severity of the injury.

"How old are you, Adams?" he asked, still staring.

"Twenty-two, Drill Sergeant?"

"Get out of my sight, Adams," he said disgustedly.

My other war wound came after we encamped in a German meadow. I burned my hand on a stove in our tent. Unlike my drill sergeant, Major Goodrich, who was the highest-ranking officer in our Public Information Office, was sympathetic.

A burn and a cut: That was the extent of my injuries.

I realized how lucky I was. I had gone to Germany, not Vietnam. I had been armed with a typewriter, not an M16.

I thanked Miss Betty for her assistance when I stalled my induction. But I regret never telling her later how much those three months meant to me.

Her son, Rick, told me he visited the Vietnam War Memorial with her in Washington D.C. many years after the war. When she recognized some of the names on the Memorial Wall, she cried.

I knew some of those names, too. Two of my classmates, Odie Gonsoulin and Billy Perkins, suffered through heavy fighting but survived. I hated that they had to go through that. And I hated the way things ended for them.

Odie was fun-loving and seemingly always on the move. That's how I remember him.

If he saw us playing badminton on our back lot when he rode by on his bicycle, he sometimes would stop by and join in the competition. He was fast enough to run on Clinton High's track team but was even quicker than he was fast.

He was probably too quick for his own good on my badminton court. Unaware of the slopes and slants of a court where experience was crucial, he often slipped in his rush to the birdie.

After a game, he was back on the move. Eventually, he changed rides – from a bicycle to a motorcycle, which became his prime mode of transportation in high school.

Odie left Clinton for the University of Southwestern Louisiana in Lafayette. He was at USL when he had his first close call.

Odie Gonsoulin in the mountains of Vietnam.

He was driving his mother's car on his way to visit his father in Sunset, La. The windows were rolled up and the radio was on. Odie never saw or heard the train coming.

It struck the car broadside and dragged it down the track. Fortunately, the train wasn't going fast. Although Miss Eleanor's car was totaled, Odie was unharmed.

His next major move proved more dangerous. He left USL and enrolled in Delgado Trade School in New Orleans with the intent of becoming a draftsman. That fit his skill set but left him vulnerable to the draft.

His draft number was too low for safety. And like so many thousands of others – through a series of random events – he wound up in Vietnam as an infantryman.

Odie did his fighting on mountainous terrain. The pictures he sent home showed him wrapped in bandages, not all of which covered the sores, which were referred to as "jungle rot," a reminder that even if you weren't waging a war, Vietnam was an awful place to be.

"It was always wet over there," his sister, Cely, said. "He was in the jungle on foot. He had jungle rot all over his arms and legs."

Odie survived that and all the deadly skirmishes with the Viet Cong. At one point, as a sergeant, he was the highest ranking soldier left in his unit.

"Everybody else (above him) was killed," Cely said. "He had to take over a command."

The Army honored him with medals and awards, but it didn't do much else for him when he returned. There was no counseling for soldiers suffering from post-traumatic stress disorder back then. You just had to deal with it – just as you had to deal with the jungle rot and Agent Orange.

"He was having a hard time with flashbacks and stuff," Cely said. "He had really bad nights. He needed counseling, but they just threw him back out there."

Odie managed as best he could. He took a part-time, low-stress job at an auto parts store to help make ends meet. He was riding his motorcycle from work on the Evangeline Thruway when an elderly man in a pickup truck veered way off course into Odie's lane.

He tried to avoid the truck, but it turned in his direction. Odie put the bike down and slid under the truck. He could have survived the broken leg, but not the lacerated liver.

He had been broadsided by a train and managed to fight his way out of Vietnam, only to be killed by a wayward driver on his way home to see his wife and little girl. He was 25.

Billy survived Vietnam and lived more than 40 years longer than Odie. But his fight didn't end when the war did.

Billy Perkins served heroically in Vietnam but paid a huge price.

"I don't think he ever got past it," said Gerald Ray Schober, who worked with Billy at the phone company for almost 30 years.

There was so much to get past. Like Odie, Billy was subjected to heavy enemy fire and saw members of his unit die around him.

"His philosophy became a little fatalistic," his brother, Tommy Perkins, said. "You never knew when your time was going to come."

That line of thinking was reinforced repeatedly.

One of Billy's duties was to patrol roads in search of land mines. His unit was about to go on duty when his captain changed its assignment for the day.

Another unit went on patrol. Three of its members were killed.

After serving with three different divisions, including the Big Red One, during his year in Vietnam, Billy returned home. He was stationed at Fort Hood when he heard the news about the Americal Division.

"A helicopter was shot down, and 34 of his friends were killed," Tommy said. "Billy had a guilt complex about that."

At times, Billy's M60 machine gun was all that stood between Billy and the enemy. Once, when he made a short jump from a helicopter to the ground, he lost his grip on his weapon. The gun separated when it hit the ground.

While dodging bullets, Billy retrieved the pin, put his weapon back together, and ran to safety. That's how close he came to not getting out of Vietnam.

He told Tommy later that the lessons he learned in childhood were what saved him in Vietnam.

When Tommy and Billy were kids, their dad had a farm worker, Vinces Dunn, teach them to hunt, fish, and track. So, even as a young boy, Billy developed skills that would prove invaluable when a low lottery number set him on the course to Vietnam.

"When I was about 8, Dad gave me over to Vinces," Tommy said. "That summer, we roamed around the woods. I learned to find tracks and learned to be aware of my surroundings – to see what was disturbed and what was not normal."

Billy later learned the same lessons, and they would help keep him alive in Vietnam. Instead of deciphering tracks, he might spot a trip wire that someone less educated in the ways of the wild wouldn't pick up.

He also had a strong sense for survival.

On one of his first nights in the field, he and a friend built a bunker three feet deep with three rows of sandbags. The rest of his unit thought they were being overly cautious and chose to sleep on the ground without cover.

But the next night, when the shooting started, they headed for Billy's bunker.

That was one of the many anecdotes he provided in letters home to his parents and brother. Tommy kept all the letters, some of which showed how Billy related his daily life in a strange, dangerous land to growing up on a cattle farm near Clinton.

"There are big, fat doves around here," Billy wrote. "Too bad, I don't have my shotgun."

Another note home: "It's not like working 24 hours in the hay field."

But nothing Billy learned in childhood prepared him for what came after Vietnam.

"He had a hard time when he started working at the phone company," Gerald Ray said. "Sometimes, he wouldn't come to work for two or three days. The supervisor kind of looked over it.

"Billy was a hard worker and really conscientious. Everything he did, he wanted to be perfect."

He could lose himself in his work during the day, but that didn't protect him from the post-war problems that plagued so many Vietnam vets.

"He didn't talk about Vietnam a lot," Gerald Ray said. "He just said, 'I had to do things that I didn't want to do.' "

Billy got through that, too. But Vietnam wasn't finished with him.

He was doused with the powerful herbicide, Agent Orange, which the U.S. sprayed over Vietnam, Laos and Cambodia from 1961 to 1971 to destroy forest cover and crops. The collateral damage was enormous and horrific.

Vietnam vets suffered a wide range of afflictions - skin irritations, psychological problems, type 2 diabetes and different forms of cancer – that were attributed to their exposure to Agent Orange.

Billy developed diabetes. His eyesight deteriorated. He lost a kidney and was on dialysis for a while. Both of his legs had to be amputated about six inches below the knee.

"Agent Orange is what did him in," Tommy said.

Arkell Merritt remembers a healthier, happier Billy and a day they spent dirt-bike racing in Chipola. On a day like that, maybe Billy didn't have to think about what was looming.

But Billy's parents, Mahoney and Janie, drove up and reminded him that he had to go for his Army physical, Arkell said. Perhaps, Billy just wanted to forget about that. I don't blame him.

For him, there was no better place for forgetting than at a dirt-bike track.

"He rode a 360cc Yamaha," Arkell said. "That was a souped up bike. Billy won a lot of races at Chipola."

He also won trophies against stiff competition in Mississippi and Texas. He became nationally ranked.

Billy's passion for racing was most apparent when he was in training at Fort Polk. He came home and raced when he had a weekend pass.

Maybe, motorcycles offered an escape for both Billy and Odie when they had time to conjure up a daydream and ride away from the chaos of Vietnam. I hope so.

They're buried at the Masonic Cemetery in Clinton. Two war heroes, two bikers – one who died too young and one who suffered too much.

Great Expectations

Charles Dickens' "Great Expectations" was required reading at Clinton High School. But another book by the same name would become more relevant for my generation.

Landon Jones' "Great Expectations," first published in 1980, was about us - the 75 million Baby Boomers who were born between 1946 and 1964.

We would have an impact on every aspect of society through our sheer numbers. And even in a town as small as Clinton, La., you couldn't help but notice. There were just so many of us.

When we began school in 1954 by stepping down into a classroom that was below ground level until we walked across a stage at graduation, we were the biggest class to make our way through the Clinton school system.

Somewhere along the way, I sensed more was expected of us, as though our greater numbers should translate into greater achievement.

Our seventh-grade class numbered more than 70 students, far more than the previous seventh-graders or the group that would follow. That was reflected in our crowded classroom.

My desk in Miss Mamie Lee Woodside's class was so close to the teacher that she could reach me with a switch. Everyone in the class realized as much when Miss Mamie Lee popped me on the ear.

I don't doubt that her punishment was warranted. But I was stunned by how swiftly and precisely she wielded the switch, almost as though she had taken a natural talent and honed it through years of practice.

Classmate Claude Rouchon said blood popped up on my ear. I'm glad I couldn't see that. And I'm sure Claude wasn't the only one who noticed.

Our class already was aware that Miss Mamie Lee towered over us. But with a switch in her hand, she loomed even larger.

Suffice to say, she got our attention. And she held it long enough to teach us something, too. After a year in her class, I had grammar down pat. For someone who had decided he wanted to be a writer, that made for a successful school year.

I don't know that Miss Mamie Lee or other teachers taught us any differently than they did previous classes. However, I do think they were aware of our potential. Maybe, teachers and coaches were intent on helping us live up to those expectations, which seemingly increased as we moved from elementary to junior high school.

But our seventh- and eighth-grade potential didn't equate to high school success in sports, which at Clinton was measured almost solely by football. There was no high school baseball team, and basketball was an afterthought.

All I remember from our senior basketball season was sitting on the bench next to coach Curtis Bishop, who agonized over the games as though they mattered. As George Taylor prepared to shoot two free throws late in a game, Coach Bishop buried his head in a towel, unable to watch.

Our football team wasn't always easy to watch, either. In both our junior and senior years, the teams were mediocre. The mediocrity was magnified by what came before and after.

Clinton played for a state championship in 1961, won the state championship in 1962 and made the playoffs in 1963. Three years after our senior football season, Clinton won another state championship.

But I still valued the size of my class.

It was customary at Clinton for eighth-graders to go out for spring football. However, because there were so many of us, coach Hubert Polk didn't include us that spring. That worked out great for me.

Given more time to think about playing high school football, I weighed the pluses and minuses. My conclusion: A 115-pound linebacker who wasn't particularly fast had little to contribute to the school's football tradition. My classmates would be better off without me.

Some of those classmates had tough acts to follow in their own family.

Claude's brother, Jerry, played a prominent role on the 1962 team. So did Billy Perkins' brother, Tommy, and Jerry Beauchamp's brother, Johnny. Warren Record's brother, Charles, was an outstanding running back on the 1963 team. Chuck Charlet's two cousins, George and Pete Charlet, also had distinguished themselves in football. George made all-state in 1961, and Pete was a backup on the state championship team.

Other classmates had high academic standards to match. Ginger Pullig's older sister, Mary Lillian; Kay Munson's older sister, Maureen; and David Brunt's older sister, Judy, were valedictorians.

Our class wasn't lacking in smart students, though. But J. Ed. Hall, our valedictorian, stood out. He not only had a high intellect, he applied himself. And he didn't need a teacher to motivate him.

When we took physics as seniors under Carey Flowers, he let J. Ed work on his own in the laboratory. I have no idea what J. Ed was doing in there, but it worked out for him. He had a distinguished career in research biology at the University of North Carolina.

Meanwhile, the rest of us spent most of our time reading the textbook and answering the questions at the end of each chapter – as Mr. Flowers instructed. Also, we had a bizarre year-long project, which required us to write a thesis of sorts on how physics would prepare us for our career.

Since many of my classmates weren't sure what their career would be, the assignment was challenging – and – probably more importantly in Mr. Flowers' mind – time consuming.

His teaching time was limited since he also did taxes on the side. And, while everyone except J. Ed was wading through the physics textbook on his own, Mr. Flowers set up an Underwood Standard typewriter on his desk and typed away.

He said he was writing a book on the 1-3-1 zone defense in basketball.

I don't know how well he could write. But he was an excellent teacher when he wanted to be. And he could coach, too, at least that's what I surmised from playing on his seventh-grade basketball team.

Like many good coaches, he wasn't lacking in confidence.

His son, Walter, was an exceptional baseball pitcher, especially if his father were nearby, according to Mr. Flowers. He once said that if he could stand behind Walter on the pitching mound, Walter would throw a strike every time.

Unfortunately for Walter, there was no baseball league that allowed a father and son to team up in that manner.

Mr. Flowers was an intimidating figure in a classroom. He was even bigger than Miss Mamie Lee, and though he never bloodied someone's ear with a switch, he was apt to throw an eraser at anyone at any time.

Neither Mr. Flowers' throwing nor Miss Mamie Lee's switching had anything to do with our success or failure. But they gave us memories that lasted a lifetime.

As I look back on my school days, things that seemed so important then seem so inconsequential now. And I realize how the little things that accumulated over 12 years formed the biggest memories.

I helped prove that by giving myself a test. After clearing my mind in a moment of solitude, I asked myself what I remembered most.

There was a ride from Clinton to Shreveport for the state FBLA convention in Coach Polk's station wagon. Every seat was taken, including the back compartment, which was occupied by Hadley Hudnall. Our suitcases were strapped to the top of the station wagon.

But they weren't strapped well enough.

Since Hadley had a rear view, he was the first to realize that.

"Hey, Coach, we just lost a couple of suitcases," Hadley said so matter-of-factly and with so little urgency that his message had no immediate impact on either Coach Polk or the other passengers.

"There goes another one," Hadley added.

By then, we were turning around to see our suitcases bouncing off the pavement into a ditch.

Another memory that came to the forefront was a speech by classmate Glancy Schmidt. I can't remember the grade. But I remember thinking how courageous Glancy was to have stepped in front of the class with not a moment's worth of preparation.

I was quickly convinced that he was making the speech up as he went along. And since I was so determined to memorize every word of my speech, I was in awe of Glancy for going from one sentence to the next without any sense of where he might end up.

I also remembered having an allergy attack in the 10th grade. After a succession of sneezes, Ginger Pullig, who was seated in front of me, arose from her desk and went to the restroom, where she washed off her perfume – concerned that the fragrance might have triggered my hay-fever attack.

Our kind-hearted homecoming queen, Ginger Pullig.

How many teenage girls are that considerate? For that alone, she deserved to be homecoming queen, which she was.

I also remembered our homecoming parade, which, as president of the Beta Club, I was expected to help plan.

The floats were constructed at the American Legion Hall the night before the parade. And they were constructed without what I considered a great deal of creativity.

After a third float was completed, I thought our work was done. Then, someone asked about the Beta Club's float.

"What float?" I responded.

That's when I learned that not only were we responsible for the parade, we also had to provide a float of our own.

Sometimes, deadline pressure can spark creativity. This wasn't one of those times.

I suggested that we stick holes in cardboard boxes, string a rope through the boxes and spray-paint the score of each of Clinton's four games on them. We would call our art work a "victory train."

I would have welcomed any other suggestions, but none were forthcoming.

The next day, I stood alone at the highest viewing point on Main Street, across from the Variety Store, as our homecoming parade turned right at the Courthouse Square. I smiled with a sense of accomplishment, convinced that I had been a factor in the worst homecoming parade in our school's history.

There was another example of my finding humor in failure when I recalled school memories.

In the 10th grade, I was selected to represent our school in geometry at the state literary rally. Although I rarely missed a question in Miss Piker's class, I wasn't brimming with confidence before the state competition. Maybe, that was because – although I was capable of preparing for the routine class exams – I didn't really understand geometry.

So it could have been a Freudian slip when I accidentally dropped my protractor into a urinal moments before the state test.

I looked at the protractor, considered my chances for success on the test and decided not to soil my hands by retrieving the instrument, even though it would be vital to solving the geometric problems.

I don't think I answered a single question on the test correctly. But when I returned to school, I assured Miss Piker how well prepared I had been. In fact, I even said I was surprised I didn't win.

I justified the lie by reminding myself what a wonderful person Miss Piker was and how nice she had been to me. It wasn't her fault that I didn't fully grasp the subject.

I used the protractor-in-the-urinal anecdote on a trivia test for our 50-year class reunion. I spoke to more than 20 classmates in gathering information for the quiz. Academic or sports achievements didn't come up that much. Instead, we talked about the little things.

Ruth Anderson got an "A" under Miss Rogers by padding her world history notebook with pages that read: "Mary had a little lamb."

Paula Morgan threw up while dissecting a frog in class, but Alice Chambers had no problem munching on a mini-pecan pie while executing the same task.

In a failed demonstration of class pride, Warren left out the "I" when he spray-painted "Senors 66" on a Clinton High School wall.

Glancy, who played an Indian in "The Mouse That Roared," prepared for the play by shooting an arrow high into the sky just before he entered the school building.

The arrow left a dent when it landed on the roof of his father's van.

Kay, who could type 120 words a minute, didn't win the state literary competition because she failed to double-space as instructed.

I guess we would have come closer to reaching our academic potential if we had been more careful. But we didn't double-space, left out "i's," and didn't consider where an arrow propelled into the sky might land.

I thought about "Great Expectations" at our reunion. Maybe, we didn't reach our potential in high school. But I was reminded how much I liked so many people in our class and how much fun I had going to school with them.

We didn't win a state championship or have an all-state football player. But we had Walter Souder, who – a few years out of high school – hitchhiked all the way from Louisiana to Seattle, drank a Coke and returned home. I wrote a column about his hitchhiking when I was editor of The Watchman, Clinton's weekly paper.

Walter still had a copy of the column when he attended the reunion. He also had clippings about other classmates and memorabilia from school. As I sifted through that, I thought, "It's as though he's a fan of our class."

So am I. And my fandom has increased through the years.

I was buoyed when I heard good news about my classmates, saddened when the news was not so good, and saddened most of all when we lost one of our classmates.

I left the reunion wishing it could have lasted longer and wishing everyone, including Glancy, had been healthy enough to attend. But in my memory, he was still there, fearlessly diving deeper into a speech whose ending hadn't been determined.

35213366R00117

Made in the USA
Columbia, SC
20 November 2018